The Big Exit

The Big Exit

The Surprisingly Urgent Challenge of Handling the Remains of a Billion Boomers

Ian Sutton

sh.

SUTHERLAND HOUSE

TORONTO, 2023

Sutherland House
416 Moore Ave., Suite 205
Toronto, ON M4G 1C9

First edition, April 2023

If you are interested in inviting one of our authors to a live event or media appearance, please contact sranasinghe@sutherlandhousebooks.com and visit our website at sutherlandhousebooks.com for more information about our authors and their schedules.

We acknowledge the support of the Government of Canada.

Manufactured in Turkey
Cover designed by Lena Yang
Book composed by Karl Hunt

Library and Archives Canada Cataloguing in Publication
Title: The big exit : the surprisingly urgent challenge of handling the remains of a billion boomers / Ian Sutton.
Names: Sutton, Ian (Canadian author), author.
Description: Includes index.
Identifiers: Canadiana (print) 20220452830 | Canadiana (ebook) 2022045289X | ISBN 9781990823039 (softcover) | ISBN 9781990823213 (EPUB)
Subjects: LCSH: Burial. | LCSH: Funeral rites and ceremonies. | LCSH: Death. | LCSH: Baby boom generation.
Classification: LCC GT3190 .S88 2023 | DDC 393/.1–dc23

ISBN 978-1-990823-03-9
eBook 978-1-990823-21-3

Contents

Preface

"Now comes the mystery!"

last words of Henry Ward Beecher,
American clergyman (1813-1877)

In the late 1940s, when I'd just turned ten in my booming railroad and industrial hometown of 10,000, our local school board was running short of classroom space. Classes had to be held in unconventional venues upstairs in our town hall, in church basements, and community halls as we awaited construction of new schools. The school system couldn't keep up with demand as returned veterans were getting their jobs back in an expanding post-war economy and producing seemingly endless litters of children. It wasn't just in our town: the world was experiencing the largest upswing in human births in history.

That explosion in the birth rate was soon referred to as the post-war baby boom, as it is to this day. It was a global phenomenon, occurring in North America, Western Europe, and some parts of Asia.

Jump forward seventy years and the reverse is now upon us. An entirely different form of accommodation needs to be considered. Those baby boomers, to be blunt, are starting to die, and all of them are going to reach their ends in the decades ahead, with the longest-lived among them expiring in the 2060s or 2070s. The question arises: what are we going to do with all those bodies?

Some might think this subject morbid or depressing. That's certainly not been my intention. The fact is that we'll all take our leave at some point. We all know it's coming; just not when. Most of us can manage to look from an honest, frank, and realistic point of view at what will happen to us after we die. One need not be preoccupied with death–psychologists call it thanatophobia (fear of death)–to consider the issues surrounding the disposal of one's body or those of loved ones. It is a fascinating and extremely important subject for all kinds of human, economic, and environmental reasons.

Indeed, the disposition of bodies, by whatever means, will prove a major challenge in the years ahead as the number of deaths increases dramatically. We've only begun to appreciate the urgency of the issue, identifying and making available alternatives to simple burial and cremation, both of which are problematic in times preoccupied with conservation and global warming. But there are a surprising number of alternatives. None is perfect, and all involve trade-offs.

The author is a Canadian and a reporter by profession for more than fifty-five years. Now in my eighty-third year, I have faced my own health issues over the several years it took to research this book, and two sisters departed this earth during the same period. Ahead of the boomers in the exit line, I feel strongly about some of the issues discussed in this book which, to my knowledge, is the first to comprehensively address the challenges of disposing of the boomer generation.

The book is written in as fair, objective, clear, and succinct a manner as possible. I have not stated preferences among alternative methods of disposition, although some appear more viable and affordable than others. I do urge readers to consider donating their bodies to medical research and encourage families to patronize independent funeral service providers in their own best interests or, as an alternative, to conduct funeral services at home, a growing trend these days.

Donations of bodies to anatomical laboratories offer a largely cost-free alternative to families, while offering genuine benefits to students, the professions, and society. But donated bodies require eventual disposition by recipient laboratories at no cost to donor families. Cremation is the usual method employed by anatomy labs at the present time, though some use a method known as aquamation.

What happens to your body after your death–a decision preferably made beforehand by the individual or, if necessary, later by family members–must be your own or your family's choice. Regulatory agencies should have no say, provided the chosen methods are legal. Nor should corporate practitioners of what Jessica Mitford called "the dismal trade" in her 1960s bestseller *The American Way of Death.* No punches are pulled in these pages regarding the funeral trade, particularly the corporate sector and its often-inappropriate behaviours and excessive profits. With any luck, the big corporations will eventually find themselves pushed to the margins of the death-care business by smaller providers offering the same services at a fraction of the cost. Already, memorial societies and co-op funeral service providers are taking root, a sure sign of progress.

The principal message of this book is that members of the public and policy makers alike need to face the new realities of life and death in the twenty-first century. There are no pat answers. The field gets more complex with the passage of time. But decisions need to be made, by individuals as well as society, and sooner rather than later.

CHAPTER ONE

What was the baby boom?

"The only thing special about boomers is that there are so many of them."

David K. Foot, economist, demographer, and
author of *Boom, Bust & Echo*

If the music people listen to defines their generation, Frank Sinatra, Elvis, and the Beatles are inseparably linked to the baby boom. Those born right after the war in the late 1940s and early 1950s were too young to remember early Sinatra or the frenzy he stirred among his bobby-soxer fans, which who probably included their parents, but he was back on top and more popular than ever by the early 1960s. Elvis, too, was shared by the boomers and those who brought them into the world. The Beatles were the great musical watershed of the epoch. Although each member of the quartet was a few years too old to qualify for membership as a boomer, they sang directly to that cohort.

It is sobering to note that Sinatra, who died at eighty-three in 1998, would have been 107 by now. Elvis would be eighty-seven if he's still around, as some like to think, forty-five years after he told his girlfriends he was "going to the bathroom to read." Half of the Beatles are gone: John Lennon by an assassin's bullet in 1980 and George Harrison by lung cancer two decades later. The two remaining members, last we heard, are in their early eighties, as are the remaining Rolling Stones, the alternative iconic rock group of the era, although its drummer, Charlie Watts, departed at age eighty in 2022.

That Sinatra, Elvis, and two of the four Beatles have now passed is a salutary reminder that boomer time is running short.

We've just passed through the worst pandemic in living memory. Even with the heroic efforts of the physicians, nurses, emergency service personnel, first responders, and elder-care specialists who guided us through the planet's most critical medical crisis in more than a century, the World Health Organization estimated that global deaths from COVID-19 reached 15 million, and more recent estimates suggest an even higher total.

Globally, the number of COVID-19 deaths had reached over 6.562 million by early October 2022. The United States by May had surpassed one million deaths from COVID-19 or its variants, the largest spike in US history. Canada, with high vaccination rates among its 38.8 million population, counted over 45,680 COVID-19 deaths by October. The United Kingdom reported 207,963 by the same month. Australia's 15,339 was a huge number in almost any other context. New Zealand reported 2,050 deaths, particularly among its older population as the country battled the Omicron strain.

While the physical, psychological, and mental toll of COVID-19 impacted many, the vast majority of its victims were older. Cruel social media messages initially described the coronavirus as "boomer remover," although it hit their parents much harder. It wasn't age alone that made people vulnerable but age-related conditions such as obesity, cardiovascular and lung disease, or diabetes. Pandemics target the vulnerable and boomers, increasingly, qualify.

COVID-19 gave us a full-dress rehearsal of what awaits millions of boomers, yet the inevitability of their demise does not really seem to have registered. For the last century, humans have lived in dangerous times, through two world wars, under the shadow of the Cold War, and persistent threats of nuclear war and chemical and biological weapons. Rogue states and non-state terrorists have been a constant menace, along with steadily rising rates of crime. And now, extreme natural disasters, exacerbated by global warming, may present the greatest threat of all. One might think these circumstances would leave us alert to the problems of managing mortality on a massive scale. But the impending demise of our largest population segment is rarely discussed.

It may simply be a function of the Western aversion to talking and thinking about death. Some of us are phobic about our mortality. But there's no evading the facts.

Every hundred years or so, wrote Bill Bryson, the author of *A Short History of Nearly Everything*, everybody gets replaced: "For you to be here now, trillions of drifting atoms had somehow to assemble in an intricate and curiously obliging manner to create you." "For the next many years," notes Bryson, "these tiny particles will uncomplainingly engage in all the billions of deft, co-operative efforts necessary to keep you intact and let you experience the supremely agreeable but generally under-appreciated state known as existence."

Two thousand years earlier, the Roman philosopher Lucretius, conceived of atoms (he called them "primal germs"). "The death of one thing becomes the birth of something else," he observed. "Things grow, and things decompose, as primal bodies enter new combinations." Your primordial atoms, writes Bryson, don't care about you at the atomic level. They don't know that you are there. "They don't even know that *they* are there. They are mindless particles." Yet "somehow for the period of your existence they will answer to a single rigid impulse: to keep you *you*."

The reasonably long human life our primal germs allow adds up to about 650,000 hours. When that milestone arrives, Bryson explains, "for reasons unknown, your atoms will close you down, then silently disassemble and go off to be other things. And that's it for you."

Dr.BJ (Bruce) Miller put it another way. "From the time you were born, your body is turning over," he wrote in a 2020 *New York Times* column. "Cells are dying and growing all day, every day." The life span of your red blood cells is just 115 days. Even at your healthiest, living is a process of dying. A vital tension holds you together until the truce is broken. "But your death is not the end of your body," said Miller, a hospice and palliative care doctor at the University of California, as well as an author who's had his own brush with death (he survived a student prank that resulted in parts of both legs and half his left arm being amputated). "The cells that held you together at the molecular level continue to break in the minutes or months after you die. Tissues oxidize and decay, like a banana ripening. The energy that once animated the body doesn't stop: it transforms. Decay from one angle, growth from another."

Unfettered, Miller wrote, the decay continues until all that was your body becomes something else. If you are buried, your atoms will live on in the grass and trees that grow where you are laid to rest, and the critters who eat there. Your very genes will live on indefinitely as long as they've found someone new to host them. "Even after interment or cremation," writes Miller, "your atoms remain intact and scatter to become other things, just as they pre-existed you and became you."

Knowing this does not make it any easier to accept. Former television news anchor Tom Brokaw, author of *The Greatest Generation* (of which he's a member), was diagnosed at seventy-three with multiple myeloma, a treatable, but incurable, white blood cell cancer (he later went into remission). "All of us objectively understand that we are approaching the end of our lives," he said, "but subjectively, it's pretty hard to come to grips with."

Television host Alex Trebek, nearing seventy-eight, was diagnosed in 2019 with stage-four pancreatic cancer, which would bring him to the end of his life twenty months later. "It makes me more aware of the fragility of life," he said while undergoing treatment, "and how very important it is to embrace life when you have it."

It requires a sturdy soul to confront the inevitable as directly as did William Shatner. The author and actor said in an interview given at the age of ninety that he wants his body to nourish a tree planted above his final resting place.

If you are granted your full 650,000 hours, you'll have lived seventy-four years and a couple of months. What happens next is most commonly described in twentieth-century obituaries as the state of having "entered into rest."

The phrase "from dust to dust," which originated in the *Book of Common Prayer* (it's not found in the Bible, as many think), is also still in use, although the Unitarian minister Robert Fulghum finds it objectionable. "We are energy, interchangeable with light," he writes in *The Rituals of Our Lives*. "We are fire and water and earth. We are air and atoms and quarks . . . we are dreams, hopes, and fears held together by wisdom and driven apart by folly. We are so much more than dust."

Whether entering into rest means that the soul will escape the body and enjoy (or not) an afterlife, or will simply rest in what the cosmologist Carl Sagan called "the long, dreamless sleep," is open to debate.

People can believe what they want. Our concern is not with the soul but with those trillions of atoms, your remains, and what becomes of them when the inevitable happens. Those of a certain age–especially those who haven't given it much thought–need to start planning.

The choices, regrettably, are not as simple as they once were. Rather, they're much more complicated, not least because we're going to have billions of bodies to handle. Most cemeteries, particularly in high-population areas, are already full and they aren't making many more of them. Ossuaries or catacombs, like the famous ones in Paris, or other traditional methods of disposal are far too limited to meet our future needs.

Cremation is increasingly popular today, but each one consumes the approximate equivalent of twenty-eight gallons of fuel and produces emissions of an estimated 540 pounds of CO_2. Consider that between seventy-five and seventy-eight million Americans, most of them boomers, are projected to reach the ends of their lives by the middle of the century and 65 to 72 percent of them currently–or are likely to–choose cremation in the absence of more eco-friendly alternatives. That will add up to an equivalent of more than 1.6 billion gallons of fossil fuels and 31.7 billion pounds of carbon dioxide going into the environment. And that's just in the United States. Similar patterns and implications are forecast for other English-speaking countries, along with other societies. The same challenges face the world's largest populations in China and the Indian subcontinent.

There is also the question of financial sustainability. Polls show that members of younger generations are less interested than their predecessors in religion and the end-of-life observances and memorialization of the departed that come with traditional faith. That attitude will only harden when they consider the enormous cost involved in conventional funeral rites and corporeal disposition. Members of Generation X and Millennials are unlikely to have the financial resources of their boomer parents, who themselves are balking at the often- monstrous sums spent on death-care. Everyone wants to do right by their deceased parents, but there are limits.

The global death-care market had reached $104 billion by 2020. It is projected to reach at least $160 billion annually by the end of 2027, with a compound annual growth rate of 4.8 percent. In the United States alone, the market is expected to hit $68 billion in 2023. Many lower- and middle-income families are already facing what's been termed "funeral poverty," an inability to cope with rising funeral costs, especially when dealing with the corporate death-care sector. There have indeed been discussions in the United Kingdom, at least at the academic level, of the need for national, government-funded, death-care programs. A public appetite for such measures may emerge as the costs of death-care escalate and become intolerable for survivors. In the meantime, the high financial costs of burial and cremation are spurring the search for alternatives.

Does that mean humans will be forced to resort to creating massive boneyards, as is already happening in some parts of the world? Will we be stacking bodies in graves? Or will we be forced to reach back in time and follow the example of the ancient Zoroastrians who simply gave their bodies over to birds, animals, and insects to devour. That's certainly not a preference, but it's not inconceivable if other new disposition methods don't become available or are not encouraged.

Society is going to have to think outside the box and adopt less land-intensive, less ecologically damaging, and less expensive methods. Fortunately, there are alternative methods available or on the horizon that meet the need for respectful, affordable, and non-toxic means of disposition. Some are imaginative and ground-breaking. Others are a bit creepy. All are contentious in one way or another.

Natural or green burials are less toxic. They make better use of available land and avoid concrete liners and steel-lined caskets; they can permit reuse of graves. Yet they, too, require land and, again, we're talking billions of bodies.

Aquamation, which basically involves dissolving the body in hot water and lye, is another option, as are "living coffins," natural organ reduction, and other disposition technologies. These don't yet have the same public acceptance as burial and cremation, but it is conceivable that they could become preferred choices when society starts recognizing the need.

All of these options and more will be required to cope with the challenge ahead. The peak of boomer deaths is expected to come around 2044, almost 100 years since the post-war birth rate first began to climb. If these people are to receive the dignity they deserve on passing, while also meeting the needs of society and the planet, a lot of work remains to be done.

CHAPTER TWO

Numbers don't lie

"We've got four decades of death coming, a lot more than we've had at any point in history."
—Carlton Basmajian, Iowa State University.

In his bestseller *Boom, Bust & Echo*, David Foot wrote that the study of human populations is the most powerful and under-utilized tool to understand the past and foretell the future. "Demographics affect every one of us as individuals, far more than most of us ever imagined," he says. "They also play a pivotal role in the economic and social life of our country." Foot, who once taught economics at the University of Toronto, says his premise applies virtually everywhere, including at the ends of our lives.

The baby boom was the most noteworthy of demographic trends in developed countries in the last half of the twentieth century. It brought that great bulge of births that shows up on a population line graph like "a pig in a python" or "a snake that swallowed a rabbit." In the United States, as boomers age, the orientation of society is rapidly changing from youth-oriented to elderly. The same applies to Canada, the United Kingdom, Australia, New Zealand, and, in fact, just about everywhere. The United Nations predicts the number of people aged sixty and above to more than double globally by 2050, with the largest and fastest increase in the number of elderly coming in the developed world. By then, 83.7 million Americans will be over age sixty-five, almost double the number in 2012.

By as early as 2030, the US Census Bureau predicts, even the youngest baby boomers will have reached their senior years and by 2035 the United States will be home to more people over sixty-five than under eighteen. The United States had almost 99,000 centenarians in 2018, a number that is expected to increase to 600,000 by 2060. This is a new experience for the United States, which until now stayed young relative to most other countries through higher fertility and strong immigration. Now, writes US Census Bureau demographer Jonathan Vespa, "Americans are having few children and the baby boom of the 1950s and 1960s has yet to be repeated. Fewer babies, coupled with longer life expectancy, equals a country that ages faster."

The same trends are taking place north of the border. A UN report showed by 2020, the number of Canadians living to over 100 grew to almost 9,000, a 76 percent increase in twenty years, while another estimate put the figure at 13,000. By 2065, Statistics Canada projects 87,500 people aged 100 or older. In the United Kingdom, the number over age 100 had reached 15,120 by 2020, while Australia hit 8,262 and New Zealand 297.

Women far outnumber men in this advanced age bracket across North America. Old age, says physician Louise Aronson, can now last a half century. "Old is only how you feel, seventy is the new fifty, 100 is the new seventy," she says.

While a rapidly aging population is new for the United States, it is not for some other countries, says Vespa. Japan has the world's oldest population, with more than one in four people already at least sixty-five years old: "Its population has started to decline and, by 2050, it is projected to shrink by 20 million people." Europe is headed down the same demographic path. Germany, Italy, France, and Spain all have populations older than the United States. Countries in Eastern Europe are even further along the slope and, within a few years, many of their populations also will begin to shrink.

Given that there are approximately 1.1 billion baby boomers in the world today, the number of projected deaths of boomers in the coming decades will be huge. The United Nations Population Division forecasts global mortality from all causes reaching 67 million by 2030. That forecast reaches 79.5 million by 2040 and continues to climb to 91.6 million by the turn of the century. Between 2020 and 2060, the years in which most boomers will meet their ends, as many as 190 million people could pass in five primarily English-speaking countries alone: the United States (134 million), Canada (16 million), the United Kingdom (28 million), Australia, and New Zealand.

Political scientist Darrell Bricker, co-author with journalist John Ibbitson of the 2019 book *Empty Planet*, says 2040 will be "the decade of departure." In the United States alone, annual deaths are projected to number 3.6 million that year. As baby boomers age, says Jason Devine of the US Census Bureau, the number and percentage of those dying in the United States will increase dramatically every year, peaking in 2055, before levelling off.

Researchers forecasts deaths of baby boomers in the United Kingdom will peak by 2045. Canada is expected to witness the cumulative demise of close to sixteen million, most of them boomers, between now and 2060. Baby-boom deaths will increase steadily until around 2054 or 2055, Statistics Canada predicts, when the youngest boomers will be in their nineties. In the remaining years, the number of deaths will stabilize.

All of these projections, of course, are based on estimates of how long people will live in the coming decades. A 2017 study by the World Health Organization and scientists at Imperial College London has projected that mortality and life expectancy will change in thirty-five high-income countries by 2030. The study, published in *The Lancet* medical journal, said these nations, including the United States, Canada, the United Kingdom, and Australia, along with the emerging economies of the Czech Republic, Poland, and Mexico, may experience longer life expectancy. South Korean is an outlier: life expectancy at birth, the report said, is forecast to reach 90.8 years for females and 84.1 years for males. By comparison, average life expectancy at birth in 2030 in the United Kingdom is forecast at 85.3 years for females and 82.5 for males. The United States posted the lowest life expectancy for those born in 2030 among the higher-income nations, an average of 83.3 years for females and 79.5 years for males, on par with Mexico.

These projections are an inexact science. There are many factors that suggest life spans can lengthen well beyond current norms, conceivably to well over a hundred years, which would delay the inevitable for many. Recently published views and data cast significantly new light on the aging process across the range of societies. Health and social care have emerged as one of the most critical factors, according to a 2020 paper in the *World Scientific Journal*. Improvements to medical care, drug therapies, and vaccines will significantly lengthen lifespans. Healthier lifestyles, in particular the drop in tobacco use, will also play a role, as will the simple knowledge that keeping busy, maintaining close ties with family and friends, and enjoying the pleasures of old age encourage longevity.

Just how much of an impact these developments will have, and how widely life-extending behaviours will be adopted, remain to be seen. Scientists already note that the death rate of people who make it to their eighties and nineties has decreased significantly in recent years. If these trends continue, we'll see massive increases in the number of super-centenarians–those living past the age of 110–in the decades ahead. In 2010, a team of researchers from Germany's Max Planck Institute recorded 1,119 individuals in ten European countries, plus Canada, Japan, and the United States, who had reached at least 110 years. The Institute's researchers reported a 99 percent probability of people reaching 124 years and a 68 percent probability of 127 years. Similarly, the journal *Medical News Today* reported new data in 2021 that projected human life spans conceivably reaching 130 by the end of the century.

To realize these dreams, says Professor Majid Ezzati of Imperial College, we must continually think about the needs of the elderly. "The fact that we live longer," he says, "means we need to be strengthening the health and social care systems to support an aging population with multiple health needs."

At the same time, there are many factors working against the promise of life extension. The Max Planck Institute reports that excess mortality among baby boomers is driven in part by what it calls "boomer penalty" behaviours at earlier ages, namely drug and alcohol abuse, smoking, HIV/AIDS, hepatitis, and suicide. Males are especially susceptible to these counterproductive choices, and more likely to be victims of homicide and reckless driving, as well. If these behavioural trends continue, says the Max Planck Institute, "it is possible that people aged sixty-five and older will experience substantial increases in mortality in upcoming years."

Poor diet and lack of exercise are still other unhelpful behaviours, contributing to high rates of obesity and hypertension. The high incidence of chronic pain among boomers is a fundamental factor in the ongoing deadly opioid epidemic which claimed more than 100,000 American lives in 2021. US boomers report being less satisfied with their health than other birth cohorts, which is further cause for concern. (Despite their complaints, baby boomers tend to be optimistic about their longevity. One survey suggests only 30 percent of Millennials expect to reach 85 to 100 years. They believe they'll live to an average 81 years. Today's boomer expects to live an average four years longer.)

Social factors matter, too. Among the reasons the United States ranks so low among the previously mentioned thirty-five nations in life expectancy is a lack of universal health care, elevated child and maternal mortality, and high homicide rates. Many of the countries in the *Lancet* study that out perform the

United States have stronger welfare systems and lower levels of income inequality. Countries that are unable to maintain a reasonably high standard of economic performance will likely find it difficult to extend lives in aggregate: health care–especially elder care and end-of-life treatments–are expensive.

Joining these behavioural and social factors in limiting lifespans are cataclysmic global events, including the recent pandemic. War has now broken out in the Ukraine, the most serious conflict in Europe since the Yugoslav wars of the 1990s. A major global conflict on par with the Second World War involving nuclear weapons would cancel all bets on global longevity.

Climate change could have a massive impact on lifespans around the world. The year 2021 ranked as one of the seven warmest years on record, according to the World Meteorological Organization, and 2022 is seeing a repeat performance. News headlines were filled with extreme weather events, from wildfires in Australia to massive floods in Europe and North America. Farmers in Siberia were desperately attempting to save their crops. In some drought-ridden western states, cattle were competing with grasshoppers for food. Boston, London, Moscow, Tokyo, and Shanghai are among the legions of cities to record new record high temperatures this year.

The high temperatures are the result of what's called a heat dome, a meteorological effect driven by the jet stream.

It creates an atmospheric bubble, preventing cooling rain or cold fronts from moderating high temperatures, and leading to extreme weather events such as heat waves and floods. Global warming exacerbates the effect.

"Climate change is making extreme and unprecedented heat events both more intense and more common, pretty much universally throughout the world," said Daniel Swain, climate scientist at UCLA. "Heat waves are probably the most underestimated type of potential disaster because they routinely kill a lot of people. And we just don't hear about it because it doesn't kill them in, to put it bluntly, sufficiently dramatic ways. There aren't bodies on the street."

More than forty million people in the northeast United States, including New York City, were under heat advisories in 2021. Halfway through the summer of 2022, seventy million Americans had been subjected to "dangerous levels of heat," reported the *New York Times*. Extreme heat has a range of adverse effects on human health, including dehydration, cramps, exhaustion, heat stroke, loss of kidney function, skin cancer, tropical infections, pregnancy complications, allergic reactions, increased risk of heart and lung disease, and mental health issues.

Frightening as floods and wildfires may be, they tend to kill tens or hundreds of people at a time. Frequent and prolonged heat waves produce far higher body counts. In June 2021, for instance, the village of Lytton, British Columbia, recorded

Canada's highest temperature ever at 49.6°C (121°F), followed by a devastating forest fire. Given only a moment's notice, a thousand people were forced from their homes. An elderly couple were the only known Lytton fatalities. But extreme temperatures persisted in British Columbia through July of that year, claiming 815 lives, over 70 percent of them seniors.

Perhaps the worst example of the effects of extreme temperatures on seniors occurred in France in 2003. August is typically a vacation month for the French. Many people, including government ministers and physicians, escape the cities for the Riviera or other relatively comfortable locales. That year, those left behind in the cities suffered through a record heat wave. More than 14,000 people died, most of them elderly. Most single-family homes and residential facilities were without air conditioning. Accustomed to relatively mild summers, many people did not know how to react to extreme temperatures, particularly the need to rehydrate. Bodies of victims weren't claimed for weeks because relatives were on holiday. A refrigerated warehouse outside Paris was used by undertakers, who lacked space of their own.

Chicago had a similarly devastating heat wave in the 1990s. Temperatures in the city reached 106°F (41.1°C) on July 13, 1995, but it felt much hotter. The heat index (relative humidity combined with temperature) went to 126°F (52.2°C). Residents were warned that the heat wave could last two days. Instead, it continued for another week. Says Eric Klinenberg, author of *Heat Wave: A Social Autopsy of Disaster in Chicago*: "The heat made the city's roads buckle. Train rails warped, causing long commuter and freight delays . . . Children riding in school buses became so dehydrated and nauseous that they had to be hosed down by the Fire Department. Hundreds of young people were hospitalized with heat-related illnesses. But the elderly, especially the elderly who lived alone, were most vulnerable to the heat wave."

By the end of Chicago's July heat crisis, more than 700 people had died, more than twice the number of deaths in the famous 1871 Chicago fire. Klinenberg attributes the extreme toll to "an increased population of isolated seniors who live and die alone." Hundreds of Chicagoans died "behind locked doors and sealed windows, out of contact with friends, family, and neighbors, unassisted by public agencies or community groups." Those who had medical problems, were confined to bed, and lacked air conditioning or access to transportation and social networks were at greatest risk.

Heat kills about 2,500 people every year in the United States and Canada alone. More people die from heat waves in the United States than all other natural disasters combined. The worst affected are the elderly and other vulnerable groups such as the homeless. Indeed, reports from Europe, the United States, Australia, and Canada have shown for years that older people die in higher-than-normal numbers during heat waves. Higher temperatures are producing what the

National Center for Biotechnology calls a harvesting effect, a short-term bump in mortality caused by weather. Summer, says Dr. Erich Striessnig of the Wittgenstein Centre in Vienna, may soon become known as "the season of death."

The more the mortality effects of extreme weather are studied, the better able we are to adapt. When the next heat wave struck Paris, notes Dr. Striessnig, authorities had emergency response plans in place, resulting in far fewer deaths. Vulnerable elderly people living alone were registered and emergency response teams either called them regularly or visited to measure their blood pressure, give them water, if necessary, or remove them to air-conditioned hospitals to receive treatment.

It was a demonstration of the human capacity to adapt, but as Striessnig adds, "adaptation can also go in a direction that makes the problem even worse." Depending on power sources, heavy investment in energy-intensive air conditioning can aggravate global warming.

That is one of the reasons mortality projections are so challenging. Many are optimistic that future societies will adapt to rising temperatures. But will it be enough, or will it simply make problems worse?

Improving future mortality depends to a large part on urban development. We are now a largely urban species. Whatever the country, cities are the worst places to live during a heat wave, with temperatures generally 10-12°F (5.6-6.7°C) higher than in rural areas. The rocklike materials of buildings and streets conduct heat about three times faster than the wet, sandy soil of rural areas. Hot air is pumped outdoors by factories, vehicles, and air conditioners as they cool interiors. Solar radiation and hot air from vehicles and buildings gets trapped between high-rise structures. There are insufficient trees to provide shade and evaporative cooling. The result is known as the "urban heat island effect."

The natural human response to an urban heat island is to crank up the air conditioner, which burns more energy and, in many instances, requires utilities to institute rolling brownouts or blackouts to avoid power outages. Governments are developing better strategies to deal with long-term urban temperature trends. More parks and trees will help, as will increased use of centralized air conditioning system and heat pumps in place of portable air conditioners, which use ten times more energy. Radiant cooling uses panels with chilled water to cool walls and ceilings. Green roofs and lighter-coloured surfaces in urban areas will reflect more sunlight and absorb less heat. Improved social services and emergency response strategies will also keep people alive.

Important as these small improvements will be to keeping people and especially the elderly alive, they are not a solution to the larger challenge of global warming. Already, more than a third of the world's heat-related deaths are attributable to climate change. A 2020 study predicts that as many as three billion people could be living in areas too hot for humans by 2070 if Earth continues to warm at current rates. A Climate Control study estimates that by 2100, land areas now home to 200 million people could fall permanently below the high tide line. These are massive challenges, and serious threats to the most vulnerable among us.

"We've loaded the dice through fossil fuel burning and other human activities that generate carbon pollution and warm the planet," wrote Michael Mann and Susan Joy Hassol of Climate Communication in the *New York Times*.

It's not like we were never warned. It is well known that the globe is already 1.2°C warmer than in the pre-industrial age and temperatures keep climbing. The editors of 230 medical journals have stated that human health is headed for catastrophe if governments don't do more to deal effectively with global warming. The impacts, they said, are becoming irreversible. A 2021 report by *The Lancet* warned that the impact on human health, especially that of the elderly and medically vulnerable, will get far worse if governments don't commit to more ambitious goals.

"There is a way out of this nightmare of ever-worsening weather extremes," say Mann and Hassol. "A rapid transition to clean energy can stabilize the climate, improve our health, provide good-paying jobs, grow the economy and ensure our children's future." But knowing what's needed is only the beginning: delivering it is the larger challenge. While governments have committed to containing global warming to 1.5°C, leaders of the world's richest democracies, the Group of Seven (the United States, Canada, France, Germany, the United Kingdom, Italy, and Japan) in early 2021 failed to agree on a timeline to end the use of coal, a leading cause of CO2 pollution, to produce electricity. A later conference of leaders from nearly 200 nations in Scotland disappointed many by its failure to stop mining and burning coal.

That does not instil confidence in the capacity of governments to meet their targets which, as scientists constantly remind us, may not be aggressive enough to protect public health in any event. One prefers to assume that humankind will eventually halt the trend towards warming of the planet, no matter how remote that likelihood may appear now, and overcome current or future pandemics, not to mention other yet-unanticipated threats to human life on Earth. Whether we do or don't will have a significant effect on the speed at which we're confronted with the problem of disposition of the bodies of aging baby boomers and other elderly populations.

To end this chapter on a more optimistic note, there are those who believe that humanity will achieve immortality and put the funeral industry out of business. Brad Partridge and Wayne Hall of the School of Population Health at the University of Queensland, Brisbane, write that one of the oldest dreams of humankind has been "to find a way to evade death for as long as possible–or even entirely." In their article "The Search for Methuselah," they note that molecular biologists, geneticists, and biogerontologists (who study the reasons behind why we age) are all actively exploring ways to extend the maximum human lifespan by slowing or stopping the aging process.

What Partridge and Hall call the "strong" form of life extension differs from "weak" form, which involves better prevention and treatment of common diseases but does not alter the upper lifespan limit of about 120 years. They've found no consensus on whether anti-aging interventions of the strong variety will prove possible. Nanotechnology, bio-engineering, and pharmaceuticals all hold promise but none have yet demonstrated an ability to improve longevity.

One of the scientists working in this field is Aubrey de Grey, a fifty-five-year-old British biomedical gerontologist and chief science officer of the SENS Research Foundation. Also the co-author of the 2007 book *Ending Aging*, de Gray promotes life extension through regenerative medicine. His ultimate goal is the eternal human. He has ideas and thera-pies, but in one published report, twenty-eight scientists said none of them had "ever been shown to extend the lifespan of any organism, let alone humans." De Grey acknowledged, "if you want to reverse the damage of aging right now, I'm afraid the simple answer is you can't."

Even if life-extension methods were to be developed, many questions would remain about their social utility. Many take the conservative position that the aging process is an integral and unchangeable part of human nature. Toying with the concept is messing with the natural order, consistent with pro-life stances on abortion and in stem-cell debates, wary of human intervention in reproduction and aging. In 2003, the US President's Council on Bioethics claimed that the human life cycle has an inherent worth and that age-extension technologies distort or pervert the "natural" or "proper" human lifespan.

Medical science has already adopted a range of technologies and treatments that sustain and elongate individual lives without running afoul of natural or divine law. The difference, the conservatives argue, is that fighting a disease or repairing damage from an accident does not interfere with the basic molecular biology of aging.

John Harris, a bioethicist at the University of Manchester, disagrees. Scientists have a moral duty to extend the human lifespan as far as it will go, he says. "When you save a life, you are simply postponing death to another point," Harris suggests. "Thus we are committed to extending life indefinitely if we can, for the same reasons that we are committed to life-saving."

There are other objections to life extension, starting with the question of who would have access to these new technologies. Would they only be available to the very rich? Would they amplify socio-economic inequities by giving the wealthy greater opportunities to entrench themselves at the expense of younger and poorer people? This is what the President's Council on Bioethics was referring to when it warned of a "glut of the able."

It has been suggested that the new technologies could merely lengthen life without any improvement in quality, leading to an escalation of health-care costs as more old people require more care. Would retirement funds be expected to carry recipients forever? And what would happen to the planet if fewer people die and women keep bearing children?

Life-extension enthusiasts answer that failing to develop new technologies for fear the rich would have first access to them precludes the possibilities that they could someday be made available to everyone. There's also the possibility that research into life extension might produce new treatments that make the later years of life more enjoyable, including less heart disease, or fewer cases of cancer or Alzheimer's. These advances may also lead to a healthier population and lower the cost of health care for all.

The debates are interesting, but they are also likely to be moot. As de Grey acknowledged, life-extension technologies simply don't exist.

The late Anglo-American writer Susan Ertz probably summed it up best. In her 1943 novel *Anger in the Sky*, she wrote, "Millions long for immortality who don't know what to do with themselves on a rainy Sunday afternoon."

CHAPTER THREE

The death of the cemetery

"Projecting the space needed for the disposal of the dead is often overlooked as a planning function."
—Carlton Basmajian, Iowa State University.

In 2010, two American academics drew attention to the coming cemetery space shortage and the challenges facing traditional burial. In their research paper, "Landscapes of Death," Carlton Basmajian and Christopher Coutts of the state universities in Iowa and Florida, respectively, review the basic boomer math.

"There's 78 million boomers in the United States alone," Basmajian pointed out. "You're talking about 3.5 to 3.7 million deaths a year in the United States, which is about a million more than we're facing right now." If all of these bodies were buried in standard burial plots, the authors suggest, it would take up 130 square miles of pure grave space, not counting roads, trees, or pathways. But there have been no major cemeteries built in the United States since about 1950, and almost no new burial-ground construction in the United States in the last seventy-five years. "We have no sense of what's coming," Basmajian says. "Like a lot of big questions, it's going to take a crisis or catastrophe before people start paying attention."

The word "cemetery" comes from the Greek, meaning, appropriately, and perhaps comforting for some, "sleeping places." They're seen as treasured sites for the memorialization of departed family members and friends, promising that here, at least, the dead will not be forgotten. Existing cemeteries are often lovely places to visit, whether or not you know any of the people buried there, but with many of them running short of space, especially in larger urban centres, it is doubtful that they can accommodate the vast numbers of bodies coming their way.

There are an estimated 145,000 cemeteries or graveyards in the United States, covering about a million acres, plus 18,000 known ones in Canada and 14,000 in the United Kingdom. Many are now closed to new burials, although open for the interment of ashes. In the United Kingdom, with a population of 67 million and a land mass of just 243 square kilometres, a 2013 survey showed half its cemeteries won't have room for new burials by the 2030s. Despite its land mass of almost 8 million square kilometres, Australia has the same problem with cemeteries reaching overload. Many are expected to exhaust their space within thirty years; in New South Wales within ten years. Roughly 170,000 Australians die each year and close to a third are buried in cemeteries.

Many attribute the problem of diminishing cemetery space to lack of foresight on the part of cemetery operators, governments (local ones in particular), and the planning profession itself. All have failed to anticipate the enormous number of deaths on the horizon as boomers die. Land for cemetery use is allocated permanently, note Basmajian and Coutts, which makes long-range land-use planning critical. But there is little contemporary guidance for planners on how to project the land land-use needs of the dead.

Erik Lees, a land-use planner in Vancouver who has designed cemeteries across the United States and Canada, calls them "the forgotten landscape." The planning profession, he says, hasn't had cemeteries on its radar, at least until recently. "I have to ask my friends in the profession 'who's been asleep at the switch for the last 30 years?' while they've dealt with employment lands, agricultural lands, housing, transportation and all those other land-use issues. Somewhere along the way they just crapped out on cemeteries. There's lots of other uses being approved on lands that we think cemeteries should trump."

Land-use demands are extreme and contentious, Lees recognizes. "You have to build hospitals and build schools and parks. But you've also got to build cemeteries," he says. As for why the planners haven't looked at the demographics and made the necessary accommodations, Lees blames the North American reluctance to think about death. "Some are very phobic about it," he says, "so it's out of sight and out of mind. But what we do with our mortal remains has become more top-of-issue in the last two to three years."

Basmajian agrees the planning and development world hasn't talked enough about the cemetery space problem. "In some regions – but not all – big dense cities like New York and San Francisco, for instance, face some real constraints because of the cost of development and the price of land," he says. "In Sydney, Toronto, Boston and London, it's not so much that they're running out of space as much as they're not really planning for what the long-term management of those spaces will be."

Basmajian worked with the small city of Perry, Iowa, to plan its cemetery needs. The town was running out of burial space but was eventually able to acquire new land. The next problem will be maintaining it. If the number of burials decreases, Basmajian points out, there'll be less money on hand to keep up public cemeteries. "We've talked to city planners in big cities and smaller places and no one had really touched this," Basmajian says. "At the local level, governments need to be thinking about how to maintain lands over time. In the United States, burial is largely unregulated, but there's still a lot of rules. The state should be setting policy to encourage local governments to consider this in their financial planning models. There may be a role for state agencies to get involved."

Laws governing burial plots in cemeteries can vary widely from jurisdiction to jurisdiction. Most cemeteries don't sell plots of land; they sell interment rights. These rights are like leases, called renewable lots. The purchaser doesn't own the ground, but has exclusive right to be buried in the plot. Owners also have the right to determine the manner of burial, usually complying with the deceased person's wishes (some cemeteries will allow a burial rights owner to pre-authorize or pre-arrange their own manner of interment). A funeral director or the cemetery authority typically deals with these arrangements after a death is registered by a physician or a registrar of death.

In many locations, the internment right is granted for seventy-five or ninety-nine years. Sometimes when the exclusive right ends, the ground is reused by the cemetery. Often, the remaining bones are removed from the grave and can be placed in an ossuary or the grave dug deeper to permit a new burial. The natural result of ground burial is the reduction of the human body to its basic elements. After several more years, there's little left but bones and teeth, but it may take fifty years before a skeleton becomes brittle and crumbles, and even longer in non-acidic soil.

In other instances, cemeteries have sold rights or leases with no expiration date. The rights are not owned by the deceased person, who can't own rights or property, but are normally held by family members. These can be renewed and passed on from generation to generation, although they usually can't be sold or transferred without the cemetery's written permission. That allows the owner(s) to keep the body of the deceased interred in the space virtually in perpetuity.

The problem of limited space in cemeteries is widespread but not uniform. Some large urban cemeteries are, in fact, underutilized. Suzette Sherman hosts the California-based web portal Seven Ponds, providing information, primarily for families, on funeral issues. She gets calls all the time from people who want to sell plots they've inherited but cemeteries won't buy them back. These city graveyards already have more burial plots than they know what to do with as more and more people opt for cremation, which is less expensive.

In the many cemeteries where land constraints are a significant issue, better use of existing space is at least a partial solution. "We're going to have to look at high density in cemeteries," says Erik Lees. That would entail reusing family burial plots after a generation or so. "After 20 years, there's really nothing left through the magic of microbiology," says Lees.

Housing stock is reused over time, but that's not yet the fashion in North American cemeteries. It is increasingly popular elsewhere in the world. The Dr. Julie Rugg of the Cemetery Research Group at York University in the United Kingdom says the only solution to the space shortage crisis is to return to the "old tradition of reusing graves." The Victorians believed that land could be reused once a person's remains had disappeared after 100 years, she told the BBC. In London, rules were introduced in 2007 to allow a practice known as "lift and deepen," with old remains removed from a grave and replaced once it's been dug deeper, allowing more burials.

An interim solution to avoid reuse is known as "created grave spaces." This involves demolishing chapels or greenhouses and clearing ornamentally planted areas. Rugg calls them "desperate measures." The funeral industry calls them "cramming."

For years, European cemeteries, including Belgium and Germany, have reused graves to save space. The British government allows bodies buried for seventy-five years to be exhumed and reburied deeper in a smaller container. A consultation in 2006 found most British people would accept double-decker graves. Burial sites in Singapore are also recycled.

Vancouver agreed in 2019 to let one of the city's cemeteries permit three or more bodies to share a single grave.

Previously, Mountain View Cemetery had to shut down after ninety-nine years of operation because it ran out of burial space. It was re-opened in 2008 with families now having the options of burying more than one body of unrelated individuals in the same grave. The cemetery can also eliminate caskets, replacing them with more sustainable options, such as shrouds separated by a layer of soil.

While most leases on burial sites in Australia are for an indefinite period, some areas are offering the option of leasing a grave for limited periods. Reusing grave sites has been legal in South Australia since the 1800s. Headstones are removed and crushed while the plot is recycled and reused.

A more extreme version of cemetery densification can be found in Vienna, a city with 1.9 million inhabitants and 550,000 graves in forty-six cemeteries. The University of Vienna's Striessnig says the graves have ten-year contracts, after which they're reused. "It might well be that this time will have to be shortened in the future," he adds. It depends on how long it takes for a human body to sufficiently decay. This method creates problems for people interested in human archaeology. If people are essentially being dissolved in lye, there may not be much for future researchers to study, Striessnig suggests. But he hopes information records will exist in other forms.

Another option gaining popularity is the standing burial, which involves placing the body upright in the grave rather than laying it to rest. This saves both money and space. Kurweeton Road Cemetery, described as "a peaceful, pastoral setting" 200 kilometres west of Melbourne, Australia, is purposely left in a natural state. For a body to be buried upright in the cemetery, it has to first be frozen rather than embalmed. It is then placed in a biodegradable shroud and interred in a plot two feet wide by ten feet deep. The cost of an upright burial is about $3,750, half the cost of a traditional burial. The four-hectare cemetery, the first of its kind when opened around 2010, has capacity for 30,000 eco-friendly burials in plots a third the size of conventional graves. The burial spaces are dug with an auger like those commonly used for utility poles. For every person buried there, a tree is planted on a nearby hill.

A related proposal in Australia would create a "burial belt" outside the country's urban areas, featuring green space with trees and even planting of vegetables. The burial belt would require natural burial, protecting wildlife and vegetation, with no embalming or conventional headstones.

At the same time as some experts worry that cemeteries are running short of space, others are questioning whether we need them at all. David Charles Sloane's book *Is the Cemetery Dead?* raises legitimate questions about conventional ground burial, pointing out that cemeteries can be wasteful and harmful, with chemicals, plush caskets, and manicured greens adding to the problem. He suggests these factors threaten the future of cemeteries and may lead them to become more environmentally responsive.

Indeed, traditional coffins are anything but green. The cheaper ones are made of plastic and fibreboard. The glue used for fibreboard coffins is a pollutant, often containing formaldehyde. Expensive traditional coffins are well built so they won't decompose. Traditional burials in the United States use 20 million board feet of wood a year, it estimates, plus 4.3 million gallons of embalming fluid, 1.6 million tons of reinforced concrete, 17,000 tons of copper, and 64,500 tons of steel. All that is in addition to the fact that cemeteries are regarded by many as poor land use and a detriment to the environment.

There is also considerable scientific research that conventional ground burial causes serious environmental contamination. Studies on the impact of cemeteries on groundwater quality began in the 1950s, but it wasn't until the 1970s and 1980s that Germany, the United Kingdom, and Canada undertook any. There is broad agreement among scientists that cemeteries produce potentially hazardous emissions. Each kilogram of a decomposing human body produces 0.4 to 0.6 litres of contaminated liquid. The leachate contains pathogenic bacteria and viruses that may "contaminate the groundwater and cause disease when used for drinking," writes researcher Józef Żychowski wrote in the *Journal of Water & Health* in 2015. The leachate also includes mineral salts, organic chemicals, and metallic compounds, including calcium, chromium, iron, manganese, and lead. The practice of embalming corpses is another source of metal pollution, resulting in leaching of formaldehyde, potassium nitrate, chromium, and arsenic. Substances used in chemotherapy, prostheses, and dental implants also contaminate the environment. By mid-2022, research had shown that COVID-19-related deaths were overfilling some cemeteries and increasing the leakage of metal pollution from graves.

"The contamination of groundwater can not only have health and environmental impacts, but also serious social and economic consequences," says Żychowski. There is a significant threat to funeral home employees and residents and animals living near cemeteries; some studies have found high levels of bacteria in wells near burial grounds. The contamination can also reduce the quality of farming and agricultural products, and leave water unsuitable for certain industrial processes and recreation. The threat is especially high in cemeteries located in low-lying lands that are flood-prone.

"Once water logs a cemetery," says Basmajian, "it becomes a huge problem that's going to get people's attention." This is another problem expected to get worse with climate change.

Yet another problem with conventional ground burial is the expense. Interment normally requires a casket, a gravesite, a memorial (such as a gravestone or footstone), opening and closing of the grave, and sometimes a vault. Especially in the last decade, costs have risen considerably. The bill can be as high as $20,000. While ground burial remains the preferred option of many people, fewer and fewer families can afford it. One recent survey found that the majority of Americans have no more than a thousand dollars in savings, which severely limits options in the event of an unexpected death in the family.

An alternative form of burial that gets the bodies out of the ground is the vertical cemetery. These have been contemplated for years and are already a trend in some regions. In Asia, bodies are buried in high-rise pagodas, including a twenty-storey one in Taiwan, where photos and urns containing a deceased's ashes are kept behind a small window. It will hold the ashes of 400,000 people. A thirty-two-storey vertical cemetery, build built in 1983 in Santos, Brazil, has space for 25,000 bodies. In Israel, to relieve cemetery space shortages, a high-rise structure added to Yarkon Cemetery near Tel Aviv can accommodate 250,000 burials. The edifice is grounded with pipes filled with earth to meet the religious requirements of Orthodox Jews. A Christian cemetery in Tughlakabad, India, built Asia's largest vertical cemetery for 300 crypts.

Notwithstanding these successes, opposition remains to high-rise burials, particularly in Europe. Verona, Italy, proposed a 330-foot-high futuristic tower cemetery but ran into opposition from citizens and politicians. A large, honeycombed skyscraper cemetery was designed (not built) by an architectural student for Oslo, Norway. It included green spaces, flowers, and trees, and featured a crane to raise caskets into high-rise chambers. Public response to the concept was mixed, at best. Nevertheless, Norway, with a population of 5.4 million, is facing a land scarcity problem. It may have to open its collective mind to these alternatives in the near future.

If the ground cemetery still exists in 2040, the decade of departure, it may be nothing like what we're accustomed to seeing today. Dr. Karla Rothstein at Columbia University's Graduate School of Architecture is the founder of the DeathLab project, a research and design space focused on reconceiving how people live with death in major cities. DeathLab's scholars, researchers, and designers are developing two projects. One is Perpetual Constellation, which uses sustainable technology for disposition and memorialization of the dead. It relies on an airless conversion of bodies to break down their organic matter and generate biogas which can be used as fuel. With a capacity of 5,400 interments a year, it would accommodate about 10 percent of all annual deaths in a typical (non-pandemic) year in New York City. Through the process, each body would be lowered into a reusable memorial vessel where decomposition will be facilitated and the energy converted into memorial lights.

The second project is Sylvan Constellation, which aims to increase the capacity of an existing cemetery, Arnos Vale, in Bristol, England. It would use technology similar to the above project to double the capacity of earth burial at Arnos Vale within six years. The cemetery was restored in 2003 and remains an active burial ground while also serving as a nature conservatory, classroom, and venue for performances and other events.

John Troyer, director of the Center for Death & Society and associate professor in the department of social and policy sciences at Bath University, was involved in developing the Future Cemetery multi-media platform, which opened in 2012 in partnership with the Arnos Vale Cemetery Trust. In his 2020 book *Technologies of the Human Corpse*, Troyer examines the relationship of the dead body with technology, both material and conceptual: the physical machines, political concepts, and sovereign institutions that humans use to classify, organize, repurpose, and transform the human corpse.

"There's a myth that people repeat: it's taboo to discuss death," Troyer says. "The exact opposite is true. We humans discuss death and dying all the time. What we don't discuss is our own personal death. We all know that death is in the future."

A goal of the Future Cemetery is to "make the future more visible" to each of us and to the general public. The project involves designers, multimedia artists, theatre programmers, technologists, computer programmers, and app creators who are transforming Arnos Vale into an open-source, end-of-life discussion; a new interactive platform for twenty-first century needs.

Technology is likely to alter our perceptions of death, dying, and the dead body, and not just at Arnos Vale. Smartphones, 3D printers, satellites, and other technological breakthroughs may mean that in the not-too-distant future, the deceased can be memorialized in far different ways than at any time in the past. Rather than burying people under granite gravestones with a limited number of words that become more difficult to read over time, future burial sites may feature QR codes or barcode squares. Visitors would scan the code to see pictures of or read about the deceased. The amount of content that could be provided is relatively enormous.

At least one academic planner regards these futurist concepts as "kind of silly, very showy and not grounded in reality." But you never know. It wasn't that long ago that a hand-held computer seemed implausible. The reason we are still here as a species is because our ancestors were able to adapt to change. If we're going to continue to stick around, we'll have to adapt in ways that take us out of our comfort zones.

CHAPTER FOUR

Cremation, popular and unsustainable

"Incineration disposes of the body in one hour in a beautiful glow of heat, and earth burial, which prolongs the process through fourteen to sixteen years of loathsome decay."
—Kenneth Iverson, in *Death to Dust.*

While it may have existed earlier, most scholars agree that cremation likely began during the Stone Age (3000 BC). It didn't begin to win wide acceptance in much of the world until early in the 1900s, and it wasn't until after the Second World War that cremation began to challenge ground burial as the way to finally go. It is now the most popular of all the disposal options, including ground burial.

The primary reasons for cremation's slow rise to acceptance were religious. Orthodox Judaism forbids cremation because it fails to comply with the religion's teaching regarding respect and dignity of the body (although many Reform Jews are comfortable with the practice). Islam strictly disallows cremation, as do some Protestant denominations, and the Eastern Orthodox and Oriental Orthodox churches, although less dogmatically.

The Church of England came around early in the last century; its most senior bishop was cremated after his death in 1944. The most significant change came in 1963 when Pope Paul VI lifted the ban for Roman Catholics. Priests were then allowed to officiate at cremation ceremonies on condition the resulting "ashes" be buried and not scattered. (They're not really ashes, but bone fragments.)

By the late 1960s, cremation was more common than ground burial in the United Kingdom, Canada, and Finland. By 2016, it had exceeded traditional burials in the United States and it has continued to do so in the years following. Cremation is expected to reach 65 percent of total US disposals by 2025 and almost 73 percent by 2030 (it is already at 75 percent in Nevada and Washington State). By 2040, the US cremation rate is expected to hit 79 percent, the National Funeral Directors Association predicts, while the burial rate will drop to less than 16 percent.

Cremation is already creeping towards 80 percent in Canada. It is over 78 percent in British Columbia and exceeding 65 percent in five other provinces or territories. In the

United Kingdom, where 37 percent of the population is over age fifty, the cremation rate sits at 78 percent. In Australia, it's 69 percent and New Zealand 75 percent.

In many Asian countries, cremation is a long-standing tradition. In Japan, it is the near near-universal option for disposition. Taiwan, Hong Kong, South Korea, and Thailand have cremation rates well above 80 percent. In India, Hindus believe burning the body frees the soul from the cycle of death and rebirth.

Is cremation the best choice for the average consumer? It depends on the priorities of the deceased and family. These are complex decisions and strong arguments can be made for many of the alternatives but, again, cost and shortages of available land are increasingly limiting options. It is expensive to acquire a burial site if you don't already own one. For many families, that alone makes ground burial cost prohibitive.

The median cost for a cremation in the United States is about $2,300. One can be had for less, depending on who provides the service, but it is also possible to pay much more. Prices can rise range to over $7,000 when including a memorial service, a casket, a hearse, an urn and other incidentals. That's a bargain compared to a ground burial, the average cost of which is just under $7,500, and often as high as $15,000 to $20,000 depending on the family's wishes and the cost of burial plots. Direct cremation through either a funeral home or an independent cremation provider is the more economical option.

Basic cremation or funeral services can cost about $1,200 (CAD) but the final price tag is often in the $12,000-to-$20,000 (CAD) range, says one British Columbia expert. "A family, if they're multi-millionaires and want to buy a $20,000 (CAD) casket and have an elaborate funeral and can afford that, they can do that," "but for most, nine or ten thousand dollars–that's a big expense."

Federal laws don't dictate any container requirements for cremation, but certain states and provinces may require an opaque or non-transparent container for all cremations, which can be a corrugated-cardboard box or a wooden casket. Many casket manufacturers provide caskets specially built for cremation. For most direct cremations, there's no need to buy a casket at all. A less-expensive heavy hardboard box, referred to as an "alternative container," is sufficient.

Some will be surprised to read that cremation caskets can also be rented. The casket is crafted with a simple inner container to hold the body. The rental casket acts as a shell around the container, making it suitable for public visitation and viewing. After the service, the funeral director removes the inner container holding the body and transports it to the place of final disposition, usually a crematorium. This rental option can cost as much as $1,600 for two days' use of the casket.

The US Federal Trade Commission's "Funeral Rule" guarantees that a funeral home cannot refuse or charge a fee for using a casket purchased elsewhere, including one bought online. If a casket is purchased online, most funeral homes will let you ship the casket to them, but they accept no responsibility for its condition on arrival. The Funeral Rule applies only in the United States, although similar regulations deal with treatment of bodies in the United Kingdom, New Zealand, and Canada.

If arranged through a funeral home, a funeral director may pick up the body, deliver it to the crematorium, and arrange for the family to collect the remains. As an alternative, direct cremation, also called simple or bare cremation, can be arranged through a crematorium. It often involves no formal ceremony. The deceased is cremated and the remains are returned directly to the family. There's no need for an expensive casket; there's no viewing, embalming, or cosmetics. Unless the family decides to bury the ashes, there's no plot or grave marker. This no-frills option costs between $1,000 and $2,200, but it requires some shopping around.

As the Funeral Consumers Alliance points out, the average cost of the cremation process is a few hundred dollars, but the consumer is likely to pay an undertaker considerably more. Because the costs vary widely, it is best to have the research complete and the choice made well in advance, when families aren't under stress.

There's an additional consideration with obese bodies. While an overweight person can be cremated, it's costly. Cremating an overweight body needs a larger retort or oven. Not all crematories will have one large enough, which means the body has to be transferred to a crematory that can handle it, resulting in greater transportation costs.

The Funeral Consumers Alliance has surveyed Americans on their disposal choices. Cremation tends to be preferred because it is cheaper and simpler. Land preservation comes up as a consideration. So does the time factor: many people are choosing cremation for their loved ones because they find the long period of decomposition in ground burials to be distasteful. The same concerns prevail in Canada, Australia, and New Zealand, especially in larger urban areas.

That people find ground burial more distasteful than cremation may be due to a lack of knowledge or failure of imagination. There is really no aesthetically pleasing way of disposing of human remains. Darryl J. Roberts, a thirty-year veteran of the death-care business, explained what happens during cremation in his 1997 book, *Profits of Death*:

"From your days in high school biology and physiology, you may recall that most parts of the human body . . . muscle tissues, flesh and organs . . . are composed primarily of water (70-80 percent), and the balance of the bones composed primarily of calcium phosphate. The application of the intense heat of cremation first evaporates the water from the body.

The flames then incinerate the muscles, flesh and organs. Most of the bone structure will crumble, but will not be reduced to 'ash' by cremation.

"The actual incineration process takes an average of one to two hours, depending on the temperature inside the retort, the condition and size of the corpse (the bodies of obese individuals give off considerable black smoke and flames when incinerated and take longer than more slender folks), and the type of container used. Once the process is complete and the oven has cooled, an attendant uses (note to pizza lovers; please excuse the following analogy) a brush similar to those used to clear pizza ovens to remove the ashes and bone fragments, and sometimes a vacuum cleaner is used. We will, here forward, use the euphemism promoted by the funeral industry and refer to these ashes as 'cremains.' The cremains are then placed in a box or in an urn purchased by the family . . .

"How much is left and what do the cremains look like? The average man, when cremated, yields approximately six to seven pounds and the average woman five to six pounds. The cremated remains are generally grey in color, but can contain flecks of other colors, created by jewelry, dental fillings, etc. If the ashes are to be scattered, the cremains will probably be passed through a pulverizing machine to grind the bones to a consistency similar to the rest of the ashes. What results has the granular consistency of sand and bears no resemblance at all to human remains . . . In the pulverization process, it is inevitable that some residue from other cremains will be mixed with others and some of the cremains will be lost, but the amounts are likely to be miniscule."

Funeral homes remove pacemakers before cremation because they can explode. Titanium hip replacements, which tarnish but don't melt, are also usually removed as they can damage bone grinders. Otherwise, metal remnants such as pins, screws, and joints that may have been surgically placed in the body are separated out of the remains, usually with strong magnets, before the bones are ground. Although some funeral homes remove old mercury dental fillings before burning the body, many states consider this a desecration of the body and do not permit it.

Most requests for permission to witness a cremation are denied, although policies vary from one funeral home to another. And, in case you were wondering, clothing for the deceased is optional. "If there's been a traditional funeral, the bodies are cremated in the clothing," says Bob Kirkpatrick, owner of A Cremation Service of the Palm Beaches in South Florida. "When there's just a direct cremation without a service or viewing, they're cremated in whatever they passed away in–pajamas or a hospital gown or a sheet." Kirkpatrick adds, "We don't do caskets. What we use is a corrugated box with a piece of plywood at the bottom to give it some strength."

While in some nations, cremation occurs in an open-air environment, the Western practice is to book a modern crematoria with one or more purpose-built furnaces known as cremators (or crematory retorts or cremation chambers). It is a relatively green method of disposal compared with conventional burial involving a metal or hardwood casket, a concrete vault, and formaldehyde-based embalming. But relatively is the operative word.

Most, but not all, modern crematories are designed to burn efficiently. During the actual cremation, the body is exposed to temperatures of up to 1,800°F (871–982°C). This process, on average, uses an equivalent of 28 gallons of fuel and produces an estimated 545 pounds of CO2 emissions to cremate a single body. Consider the pollution to come as more than seventy-two million Americans are projected to die over the next twenty to fifty years, most of them from the boomer generation. If 70 percent of them choose cremation, that will add up to an equivalent of more than 1.4 billion gallons of fossil fuels burned and 27.5 billion pounds of CO2 produced. Again, those numbers are for the United States alone.

Not all crematories are the same. The environmental impact depends on the type of facility in which the cremation takes place, says Laura Green, senior toxicologist at Green Toxicology in Brookline, Massachusetts. The typical crematory in the United States, she says, is part of a funeral home with one or two retorts. The primary emissions are carbon monoxide and fine soot, but sulphur dioxide and trace metals may also be produced. Larger, more sophisticated operations will funnel cremation after-gases into wet scrubbers or very large filters to reduce emissions. These methods of filtration can't eliminate all pollutants but pollution is minimized, almost to the point of being inconsequential, says Green. Smaller facilities tend to be equipped with so-called cyclone systems to control pollution, but they only deal with particulates, leaving combustion gases untreated. The design of the retort, the height of the exhaust stacks, and the way in which the crematory is operated will also influence the amount of pollution it produces.

In some states, crematories can only operate in grave-yards; they can't be added to a community funeral home. If a funeral home wants to offer cremation to its clientele, it has to do it in a separate facility.

"The thinking apparently is it's better to have bad air in a separate facility, because no one lives there, dealing with the dead," says Green, "and it should only happen in one place, whether you're going to bury or burn them." Anyone who wants a better sense of the environmental impact of cremation at a particular facility had better be prepared to ask questions. "Like all things, there are good ones and bad ones," says Green. "Whether there should be better federal regulations is a good question."

Given the demand for cremation services, new crematoria will have to be constructed and existing facilities expanded.

In North America, there are no national requirements that crematoria be kept at distances from residential areas. Crematories are regulated at the state, provincial, or territorial level. And it's the regional or municipal authorities that determine whether minimum setbacks are required based on planning and environmental considerations. That leaves cities and towns answering questions about health risks to their residents, who generally oppose crematories anywhere near where they live.

How worried we should be about the siting of crematoria is difficult to say. There are few studies of how their emissions affect local air quality and whether they have an impact on local health. Some countries have set specific air pollution regulations for emissions of pollutants from crematoria, using ambient air quality criteria for identifying pollutants, but attributing emissions to a single source is not always accurate. The World Health Organization and US Environmental Protection Agency advise that care be taken to limit exposure, particularly to vulnerable populations such as infants, children, pregnant women, and the elderly. Most local governments permit crematoria in conjunction with cemeteries or in specified industrial zones, with minimum distances separating them from schools, daycares, libraries, and care facilities. But not all jurisdictions dictate and enforce setback distances, leaving the siting of a crematorium to the discretion of local officials.

Meanwhile, the debate over whether cremation is an environmentally responsible means of disposing bodies continues. It is reasonably well established that flame cremation does less harm to the environment than having a body full of formaldehyde buried in a concrete vault. But as Nora Menkin, former executive director of the People's Memorial Association in Seattle, told *National Geographic*, "cremation takes up about the same amount of energy and has the same emissions as about two tanks of gas in an average car. So, it's not nothing."

Green burial advocate Mary Nash says people need a better understanding of what cremation does in terms of environmental damage before making their choice. She's had people tell her, "'Oh, I'm going green, I'm going to be cremated.' You have to disillusion them and tell them, no, that's not going green. It's about the worst thing you can do. Cremation is pretty bad."

The Funeral Consumers Alliance recommends people choosing to cremate a body use more efficient containers, such as a cardboard or cremation caskets, or simply a shroud. To offset the carbon produced by cremations and minimize global warming, some funeral homes invest in wind or solar energy, while others plant trees to compensate for carbon emissions, it says.

A study by Dutch scientist Elizabeth Keijzer maintains that while cremation is an obvious source of carbon emissions, it has environmental advantages over burial, largely because of reduced impact on land use. Putting the choice in perspective, she notes that cremation or burials account for only a quarter of the environmental impact of the average funeral. The carbon emissions produced by those attending a funeral tend to be far greater.

Ed Bixby of the Green Burial Council believes there are more eco-friendly ways to dispose of a body than cremation but recognizes that for many families it is the affordable option. "We realize that individuals and their families have to make hard decisions and that sometimes comes down to dollars and cents and they have to choose cremation," he says. "We're saying that we can't advocate cremation, but if you opt for cremation, you've done what you need to do and we respect that."

While this chapter has primarily dealt with the impact of mass cremation in the West, many countries share the problem. In India, the age-old tradition of cremating relatives outdoors on pyres has led to cutting down tens of millions of trees each year. It also contributes to air and river pollution, since most cremations take place near the banks of the Ganges. Since 1992, the non-profit Mokshda Green Cremation System has tried to minimize pollution by giving communities access to metal pyres that use less than a quarter of the wood usually required for funerals. Close to fifty pyres are spread around nine Indian states. A single metal pyre can handle as many as forty-five cremations daily, reducing the amount of wood needed to just that required to cremate the body. More than 150,000 cremations have taken place on Mokshda pyres, saving over 480,000 trees and 60,000 metric tons of ash from rivers and releasing 60,000 fewer metric tons of greenhouse gas emissions. The system has received inquiries from countries in Africa and Asia.

Scattering ashes of the deceased in a special place is increasingly a popular choice. Cremation ashes are sterile and organic matter, so it's safe to disperse them in the environment. To mitigate the environmental impact of flame cremation, some people use special urns in which remains can be mixed with an organic medium to support plant growth (cremated remains can't support plant life on their own). There are no prohibitions on scattering ashes on one's own land, providing it doesn't impact adjacent land use or streams.

Provided it's permitted by local authorities, a scattering ceremony can take place in a meaningful location. Some find it hard to simply pour ashes on the ground or in the sea. A funeral director can help create a meaningful ceremony. Finding the right location requires preparation. Some state and provincial regulations prohibit scattering in certain environments. While scattering at sea is permitted, there are federal regulations. Some, but not all, cemeteries permit scattering. These regulations are published or should be checked with a government agency, or the landowner's permission sought.

CHAPTER FIVE

The pros and cons of green burial

"It's a choice not to do harm, and it's a choice to add value to the earth in our death."
—Ann Hoffer in *Natural Burial Cemetery Guide*

Green burials are seen by their proponents as a way to depart earth with an act of kindness to the environment. In a nutshell, a green burial means the body must be in its natural state to permit natural decomposition. It is also known as natural burial and it is considered an eco-friendly alternative to six-feet-under in a conventional cemetery. Its advocates strive to live their lives in harmony with nature; by enabling the natural processes of decay, they see themselves dying as they lived.

Regrettably, many people don't understand what green burials entail. A study conducted by researchers at universities in Kansas and Manitoba discovered that half of people over age sixty who were environmentally active didn't know what green burial was all about. "We essentially don't have too much information to guide us as scientists, much less for older adults, as to what is the greenest way of taking care of one's remains," said Paul Stock, associate professor of sociology and environment at the University of Kansas. His research partner, Mary Kate Dennis of the University of Manitoba, adds: "Some of the environmentalists in our study didn't know there were laws that say they can be buried on their own land."

In an introduction to her *cemetery guide*, journalist Ann Hoffner writes that the movement weighs the consequences of its actions on the world. Many believe green burial was how Americans buried their dead until the Civil War, when modern embalming techniques were developed. "But modern green or natural burials have a different emphasis," she writes. "It is a deliberate choice, an option to conventional burial." It can secure land in its natural state for years to come. "It's a choice to do no harm, and it's a choice to add value to the earth in our death."

The Green Burial Council in the United States is the primary authority on green burial in North America. It acknowledges there's much debate over the use of the word "green" when discussing interment and that different people have different ideas about what qualifies as a natural disposition. Broadly speaking, a burial grounds can be considered green if it meets the following criteria:

- Caring for the dead with minimal environmental impact that aids in the conservation of natural resources.
- Reduction of carbon emissions.
- Protection of worker health.
- Restoration and preservation of natural habitats.

Natural as well as hybrid cemeteries (offering both natural and conventional interment) that follow these practices fall under the general category of green cemeteries. Also covered are conservation burials, which are natural interments on conservation lands. Groups in the United States, the United Kingdom, Canada, Australia, and New Zealand are buying up land to conserve it for nature and human body disposition.

More particularly, green burials involve nothing in the way of formaldehyde embalming or concrete burial vaults or varnished mahogany caskets. They use biodegradable caskets or shrouds. If a casket shell is used, the Green Burial Council instructs that it be made primarily from reclaimed, recycled, or renewable materials that are biodegradable under burial conditions. Wicker, bamboo, and cardboard are popular options. Casket liners, fasteners, and handles must also be made from material acquired in an eco-sustainable manner.

It follows that plastics, acrylics, or similar synthetic materials are banned at green burial sites, as are adhesives that release toxic by-products in their manufacture. The coffin must be produced in a sustainable manner that conforms to fair trade practices (and greenhouse gas emissions produced by transportation of the coffin and the body must be offset by enviro-friendly measures). For many green burial advocates, a cloth, natural fibre, or a shroud is preferable to a coffin. These can be purchased far in advance and are easily stored.

Often there is no need to use heavy equipment for burial in a green cemetery: the grave is part of reclaimed land or forest. "If you're going down green," says Canadian expert Susan Greer, there is no tombstone and freshly mown grass treated with pesticides. Graves are located a safe distance from drinking water sources. Grave markers may be natural fieldstones, or none at all. For those who wonder, animals haven't caused a problem for natural burials. In more than twenty years, there's been no sighting of animals disturbing a natural grave. Their eighteen-inch depth is enough to discourage their interest.

Death-care consultant Shane Neufeld, who's managed, been employed by, or owned funeral homes for thirty-one years, thinks the term "green burial" needs to be more clearly defined. It is in danger of becoming a "buzz word" and "a bit contrived." Being buried without a casket or embalming could be where being green ends, he suggests: "Digging a hole and putting a body into it is pretty green."

Purists want to take the definition of green burial further and outlaw fossil fuels, which rules out taking the body to the cemetery by automobile. "Do you ask your friends to pick up a shovel or will your use a backhoe that uses diesel fuel?" asks Neufeld. There's nothing green about a backhoe, but digging a grave is hard work that can take up to four hours. Families need to decide what they believe reasonably constitutes a green burial and just how natural they want to be.

However the grave is dug, the Green Burial Council emphasizes safety. If by hand, the council says an experienced gravedigger must be in charge and provide a safety overview and proper equipment for the diggers. If a backhoe is used, the operator must be experienced and the area restricted to the operator and qualified assistants.

Ed Bixby, president of the Green Burial Council, operates half a dozen cemeteries in the United States. Among them is the natural burial Steelmantown Cemetery in New Jersey, the state's first natural burial preserve. As a conventional cemetery, Steelmantown had fallen into disrepair. Bixby acquired it for one dollar from its previous owners in 2007. It now brims with flowers and other greenery. A single plot in the historic section of the cemetery costs $1,500. A double plot in its woodland area is $3,000. Burial with a shroud runs between $100 and $300.

Bixby has been restoring historic cemeteries ever since. A former real estate broker and land-use expert, he is regarded as a leader in the natural burial movement. Among his companies is Destination Destiny, a full-service alternative funeral provider that also arranges life celebrations and memorial event planning (it will even make travel arrangements for attendees). A marina and sea skiff owner, Bixby also takes families off the New Jersey coast to scatter their loved ones' ashes. "In death," he says, "you should still be able to care for your loved one and in a way that feels like they belong to you."

Bixby especially likes to advise families to memorialize the lives of loved ones by planting trees. "The best way I can explain that," he says, "is if you were to plant an oak tree, which has a very long life, what would the carbon offset of that tree be? If it was fortunate to live for more than 500 years, that carbon offset would erase the carbon footprint, not only of the cremation, but of the life that individual has lived."

By one recent count, the United States has more than ninety registered green burial cemeteries and memorial woodlands, regarded as natural burial sites. There are many more hybrid cemeteries. In the United Kingdom, almost 300 sites are designated as natural burial grounds, the first of them established in 1993. The Association of Natural Burial Grounds in the United Kingdom, created in 1994 to help people establish sites for green burial, provides guidance to natural burial ground operators and a code of conduct for members. One of its provisions requires that families be allowed to organize funerals themselves without the services of a funeral director if they wish.

Choices available to the family range from simply wrapping the body in a shroud before it's interred to organizing a memorial service. Oona Mills knew just what to do when her grandmother died in 2018. "She was a natural gardener for most of her life and lived very minimally," she said, "so it seemed very fitting for her to have a natural service, especially since she'd told me that the greatest achievement in her life was the compost that she'd made." Mills' woodland service, she told *The Guardian* newspaper, aimed to keep the burial as low-tech as possible, using a wicker coffin and no embalming fluids. "Natural burials are very effective," Mills said. "You can bury someone at three feet rather than six feet under, which is much quicker for the body to decompose."

Until recently, there were only two Canadians provinces that had full green-burial sites: three in Ontario and two in British Columbia. Most other Canadian provinces or territories nevertheless permit green burial. That's an issue the Natural Burial Association of Canada actively addresses.

"We're trying to build awareness that it's legal," says the association's executive director, Susan Greer, "because a lot people think it isn't." People need options at end of life, she continues. There are limits to how many bodies conventional cemeteries can hold, and if cremation is seen as the only alternative, it becomes a carbon pollution issue. "People don't know that cremation is so eco-unfriendly, so we try to build awareness of that."

Some Canadian cemetery bylaws insist that a vault be used, says Greer, which disqualifies them as natural burial options. In fact, there is no legal requirement in Canada to use a vault. Families can buy a biodegradable box or a heavy corrugated cardboard box.

A survey by the National Funeral Directors Association in the United States found almost 54 percent of Americans are considering green burial. More than 70 percent of cemeteries report an increased demand for natural burial. Cost is one factor driving the demand. Burial in a green cemetery or natural preserve can cost between $1,000 and $4,000, which includes the plot, opening and closing of the grave, and a one-time fee for perpetual care. A natural plot in a hybrid cemetery is generally the same price as a conventional plot but the savings on embalming, coffins, and vaults can run over $8,500. As for the environmental cost, a green burial, over a normal fifty-year cycle, produces about as much carbon as driving an average car for three months. That's one-tenth the amount of carbon produced by a traditional burial.

The entertainment industry has also played a role in popularizing green burials. Advocates credit HBO's "Six Feet Under" with mainstreaming the concept. The series, which ran from 2001 through 2005 and was widely regarded as one of the greatest of all time, followed the often-dysfunctional personal lives of a fictional family in the funeral business. The sensitive depiction of the green burial of Fisher, one of the principal characters, showed the process to be a deeply moving experience for those mourning him. The episode did more to sell the idea of natural burial to the public than media coverage of the topic was able to manage. The web portal Grave Matters lauds executive producer and writer Alan Ball's "compelling script" and the character of Nate Fisher, "the show's dazed, confused, but ultimately decent free-thinker who's laid to rest six feet under–in the most natural of ways."

There is obvious tension between the traditional cemetery industry and the green burial movement. Josh Slocum of the Funeral Consumers Alliance says the reaction to natural burial was as bad as when funeral directors first confronted the growing popularity of cremation in the 1960s. Experts in green burial, at least get invited to funeral trade conferences, he says. But natural burials aren't big money-makers for the industry. Often cemeteries will only begin to offer green burials in response to public pressure.

"After all," writes Slocum, "green burials are what you don't buy."

Funeral directors may be tempted to discourage them simply because they reduce cash flow. In their joint study, published in the journal *Mortality*, researchers Stock and

Dennis also attribute the slow acceptance of green burial at least in part to the profit-driven funeral industry, although they note that family and religious considerations also play a role.

As the practice of green burial has become better known, advocates have been alarmed by an upsurge in "greenwashing," the making of false or misleading claims about environmental impacts. The Green Burial Council sees a "greenwashing epidemic" by the death-care industry. Many suppliers are offering services that only masquerade as green burials. The Council has petitioned the Federal Trade Commission to develop stricter standards for claims of environmentally friendly funeral services and methods of disposition as part of its updated Green Guides.

The Green Burial Council revised its own cemetery standards in late 2019 to clarify and improve standards for natural and conservation burial grounds. It has created certifications for every aspect of death-care, including burial products, funeral homes, and burial grounds. It wants people shopping for end-of-life services to be wary of unverifiable claims and certifications that are financially tied to companies pushing supposedly green products.

Cemeteries that practice green burial across the United States are listed in the Natural Burial Cemetery Guide. While the guide doesn't endorse one cemetery over another, it helps readers make their own informed decisions. Regularly updated with new cemeteries, the guide can be ordered from greenburialnaturally.org. Or visit nhfuneral.org for another up-to-date list of green and hybrid cemeteries in both the United States and Canada compiled by the New Hampshire Funeral Resource.

CHAPTER SIX

Reverend Tutu's choice

"Dying people should have the right to choose how and when they leave Mother Earth."
—Archbishop Desmond Tutu, primate of the
Anglican Church of Southern Africa

Aside from green burial, many regard alkaline hydrolysis, a relatively new technology for human body disposition, as conceivably the gentlest way to depart the earth. Unlike other methods, it requires no use of valuable land and, unlike cremation, it has a negligible environmental impact. But, as with the fire of cremation, this water-based method happens swiftly. It basically dissolves the body in a mixture of heated water and lye.

In addition to its technical name, alkaline hydrolysis (AH) is known by trade names: Aquamation and Resomation. It is also commonly referred to as water resomation, aqua-cremation, biocremation, chemical cremation, and flameless cremation. While some of those terms may not be technically accurate, as we'll see, they depend a lot on the legal interpretation of the term "cremation."

Whatever its label, the method may become one of the most widely accepted default alternatives to flame cremation. Microbiologist Sandy Sullivan, who formed the UK-based Resomation Ltd. in 2007, says the process uses five times less energy than flame cremation and reduces greenhouse gases by 35 percent. Bio-Response Solutions, which manufactures the equipment in the United States, makes similar claims.

The body of late Nobel Peace Prize laureate Archbishop Desmond Tutu underwent the process at a service in Cape Town, South Africa, in January 2022, following his death from cancer. Revered for a lifetime of work for racial justice, the ninety-year-old anti-apartheid champion wanted an environmental-friendly funeral, devoid of ostentation. Reverend Tutu's final wishes set a compelling example for anyone concerned about the planet.

Since the Reverend Tutu's funeral, Indiana-based Bio-Response Solutions has seen sales of its pricey machines almost double. Joe Wilson, its CEO, says the company had typically received an average six orders a year but in early 2022, that had increased to ten units and could continue to grow. Tutu's decision, Wilson says, was "very" influential. He predicts it's likely to influence the Catholic Church to endorse the technology, similar to what happened when Pope Paul VI lifted the ban on cremation in 1963.

"It's going to put tremendous pressure" on the Catholic Church, Wilson says, because of the affiliations Tutu had with Christian doctrine and environmental protection. "He basically put the world on notice to choose an environmentally sound process. He was all about the environment." Tutu's disposition is also going to put pressure on some states, says Wilson, which "now see that it's for real and they really have to do something."

Wilson's optimism, naturally, is in line with his business objectives. There remain significant religious, cultural, and regulatory hurdles in the way of widespread adoption of alkaline hydrolysis. But, first, a closer look at the process.

Originally developed to convert animal bodies to plant food, alkaline hydrolysis was created by British chemist Amos Herbert Hobson, who obtained the first US patent for it in 1888. The alkaline hydrolysis/aquamation machine is an air- and water-tight chamber. The body is placed in a rigid stainless-steel basket, inserted in a pressurized, stainless steel tube-shaped vessel filled with water and an alkali solution of potassium hydroxide and caustic soda. The vessel is sealed. The body mass, gender, and weight of the deceased determine the amount of water and alkaline chemicals. The high-temp/high-pressure unit uses about 250 to 300 gallons of a coffee-coloured liquid that's flushed down the drain with about 65 gallons of liquid bodily remains. The effluent is a peptide soap which flows out with wastewater.

The decomposition that takes place is the same as with natural burial; the process is simply accelerated with chemicals, heat, and a certain amount of agitation. The web portal In The Light Turns (inthelightturns.com) compares alkaline hydrolysis to ice melting in a glass of water. With warm liquid around it, ice gradually disappears, writes founder Susan Fraser. Under higher temperatures, often with pressure and agitation, liquid cremation causes the soft tissues of the body to melt. The heat neutralizes diseases and contaminants. It also uses a quarter of the energy caused by flame cremation, with lower emissions.

The process can take a few hours to most of a day, depending on whether the high- or low-temperature equipment is used and the person's body mass. All that remains in solid form are the skeleton and teeth, which resemble a white powder after being dried and pulverized, amounting to about 32 percent more material than with flame-based cremation.

Mercury teeth fillings are disposed of in an environmentally safe manner, unlike flame cremation, where they sometimes go up the smokestack then fall back to the earth as a contaminant. As with cremation, the pulverized bones are returned to the family, along with metal or electronic parts such as pacemakers and artificial joints. When possible, stainless steel and titanium implants are recycled.

Wilson, who has worked forty-four years in biological industries, says his company designs and builds both types of units for use in the United States and many other countries. (A high-temperature unit was used in Archbishop Tutu's funeral.) The equipment is expensive, with high-pressure machines costing up to $400,000, significantly more than the low-temp units. The higher temperature/pressure system processes the body at 160°C (320°F) over four to six hours, fast enough to process multiple bodies in one day. Low-temperature machines use 98°C (208°F) degrees over fourteen to sixteen hours. Training is required to use both kinds of machine.

The benefits and safety of the different methods are subject to some disagreement between manufacturers in the United States and the United Kingdom. Microbiologist Sandy Sullivan launched Resomation Ltd. in Glasgow, Scotland, in 2007. It builds only high-pressure units. Sullivan refuses to use the low-pressure option. He claims his technology is "a totally different beast" from Wilson's Bio-Response units sold in the United States, Canada, and several other countries.

In addition to being three or four times as fast, Sullivan says his equipment produces a better "quality of ash" at the end of the process, benefits that he says justify the greater expense. "I'm happy to have competition," he says, "but I absolutely don't believe in low pressure." Proponents of the low-temp, low-pressure systems maintain that there is an increased danger with the high-pressure, high-temperature alternatives. But Sullivan insists his machines are "foolproof, and safety is built into it to the nth degree."

The low-temperature process is holding sway in most jurisdictions, primarily in North America. They are less expensive for funeral homes and they use much less energy–about 85 percent less than cremation. Solar and wind power can be used to heat the water for the units.

The price of alkaline hydrolysis to the consumer is similar to flame cremation, between $1,200 and $1,600. But while the equipment has a greater upfront cost, the consumer price will likely drop as it becomes more popular. A study conducted by a university in the Netherlands examined three methods of disposition of human bodies–burial, flame cremation, and alkaline hydrolysis–and their respective impacts on the environment. It concluded that green burial and alkaline hydrolysis have the lowest environmental impact.

Drew Gray, a funeral director in Prince Albert, Saskatchewan, was the first to offer alkaline hydrolysis in Canada. It is now preferred by most of his customers, he says. He intended to offer cremation, but zoning regulations wouldn't allow a crematorium. That led him to Indiana, where he ended up buying a low-temp/low-pressure unit from Bio-Response. "I'm a real advocate of it now," Gray says. "We've had a fantastic experience." He conducts a hundred funerals a year with alkaline hydrolysis and the number is growing. He's even changed his own pre-arranged funeral to use the procedure.

Sandy Mahon, registrar of the province's funeral regulatory agency, helped Gray obtain his licence for the low-temp aquamation unit after consulting an engineering study on the technology. The study found that the effluent from the process is basically peptide soap and ammonia. "It's beneficial to the wastewater system because it kills bacteria inherent in the system," Mahon says. In one case, a firefighter chose Gray's system for his disposition preferring it over flame cremation.

The Cremation Association of North America (CANA), among others, agrees that alkaline hydrolysis is an environmentally gentler process than either flame cremation or ground burial, using significantly less fuel and delivering less of a carbon footprint. CANA prefers the technical term "alkaline hydrolysis" to any of the trade names or euphemisms because it clearly describes what happens, using water to break chemical bonds. Notwithstanding the water, CANA insists that alkaline hydrolysis is a form of cremation. "The body goes in," she says, "bone fragments come out."

CANA was following the lead of legislatures in accepting the new process. As US states and Canadian provinces began to legalize alkaline hydrolysis, says Kemmis, their laws expanded existing regulations to define alkaline hydrolysis as a form of cremation. CANA recognized the trend and in 2011 chose to agree that cremation is simply the process of speeding up decomposition, traditionally done with fire but also through methods like alkaline hydrolysis. The broader definition includes any "mechanical and/or thermal or other dissolution process that reduces human remains to bone fragments." CANA was the only trade association to take this controversial position, says Kemmis. *Webster Dictionaries* define "cremate" as reducing bodies to ashes by burning. "Because alkaline hydrolysis doesn't burn, people claim it's not cremation," she says. But cremation is not defined by dictionaries, Kemmis says: "It's defined in legislation."

Alkaline hydrolysis was approved in 2003 by the Minnesota State Legislature and the first single-unit alkaline hydrolysis machine went online at the Mayo Clinic three years later. Mayo was the first facility in the United States to use the process for bio-cremation of human remains. Anatomy labs at the University of Florida, University of Texas, and UCLA dispose of donated bodies through alkaline hydrolysis and by grinding the bones to dust and then scattering them two miles offshore, forming white rings that float away and sink in the Pacific.

By 2022, twenty-five states had legalized alkaline hydrolysis, with legislation pending in the State of Hawaii. Several additional states, including Texas, Arizona, Virginia, and potentially New Jersey and New York, are considering it, especially since Tutu's funeral, and still others are considering broadening their definition of cremation to include his preferred method.

The process has also been approved in the Canadian provinces of Ontario, Quebec, and Saskatchewan. In British Columbia, a petition calling for its legalization has gathered several hundred signatures. It is also legal in the United Kingdom, Australia, New Zealand, Mexico, and, more recently, under review in the Netherlands and South Africa. Advocates believe the market in South Africa will almost certainly grow as a result of Tutu's decision.

Notwithstanding the legalization of alkaline hydrolysis, some US states lack an operating provider, says CANA. The nearest could be in a neighbouring state. Also, regulations vary from state to state. Some require funeral homes to have hazardous material companies dispose of the remaining liquid, although water treatment authorities generally like the effluent coming into their systems, since it's sterile and contains amino acids, peptides, potassium, and sodium, which actually help clean the water. "There is no tissue and no DNA left after the process is complete," says CANA. "The effluent is discharged with other wastewater and is a welcome addition to the water systems." Some experts say the liquid by-product could be used to fertilize gardens because of its potassium and sodium content, one of the reasons the method is referred to it as "green cremation."

But there are still hurdles. While the high-temperature method of alkaline hydrolysis is recognized by the World Health Organization and the US Centers for Disease Control as a safe and sustainable technology, the low-temperature method is more controversial. In 2019, the American microbiologist Gerald Denys authored a peer-reviewed study that found the low-temp process as effective as the high-temp alkaline hydrolysis method for use on animal and human tissue. Indeed, it exceeded the sterility requirements of US state and territorial alternative treatment technologies. The process, Denys said, validated destruction of prion-sized particles, including those from progressive neurodegenerative disorders that can affect humans and animals, among them Creutzfeldt-Jakob Disease. Still, not everyone is convinced.

The registrar of the Bereavement Authority of Ontario (BAO) insisted more than two years ago that more research was required on low-temperature alkaline hydrolysis. Contrary to the position of the Cremation Society of North America, registrar Carey Smith wrote in a 2020 blog that alkaline hydrolysis "is not cremation." It is marketed as a lower-cost option to families and businesses for disposition of the dead, he said, but there is no scientific evidence that low-temp processes destroy prions, as high-temperature alkaline hydrolysis does.

Microbiologist Denys stated succinctly that Smith was "misinformed." But that didn't stop the BAO registrar from forging ahead. A funeral home in a Canadian town had a three-year legal confrontation with the Ontario regulatory agency over its low-temperature alkaline hydrolysis service. The position of the BAO drew significant media attention, including in funeral trade publications which viewed the BAO's stand as potentially arresting the adoption of the new technology.

After dropping hundreds of thousands of dollars in legal fees and forfeited revenues, the funeral home owner, Trevor Charbonneau, obtained three rulings from an appeal tribunal which overthrew the BAO's decision and ordered his license reinstated. The tribunal based its rulings in part on research from a Denys's study and its determination that the process posed no threat to human health.

Regardless, the registrar of the BAO has continued his campaign against alkaline hydrolysis (his board of directors appears to be looking the other way). Some smaller funeral homes believe the agency is overstepping its authority and demonstrating a lack of concern for bereaved families by limiting their choices for disposition of loved ones. Pat Ottmann of *Canadian Funeral News* described the BOA's response as "the overbearing arm of government bureaucrats imposing a ton of pain on independent business people." An American industry journal, *Connecting Directors*, wrote that the Ontario case "reads like a bad novel with a looping plot line."

"Nobody's listening to Ontario anymore," says Joe Wilson, who claims to have negotiated an agreement to provide Ontario with low-temperature machines despite the BAO's obstructionism. "Ontario lost a lot of credibility by pulling that crap." One of the great advantages of low-temp, he adds, is that it uses none of the intense pressure that poses a danger with high-temp machines. "With low temperature, you can open the door and watch it . . . it's that safe. There's no microbial action, we use less water, less energy and less alkali with low-temp. What's important is that we use less resources."

Another form of opposition to alkaline hydrolysis has come from the religious community. New Hampshire approved the process for use in 2006, only to have it rejected two years later, and again in 2013, under pressure from church groups. State Catholic Conferences in New York and Ohio have opposed alkaline hydrolysis. It also still remains illegal in Indiana, where, ironically, the machines are produced by Wilson's company. One Indiana state representative, who successfully voted against the bill to legalize it, owns a casket business, which may be relevant. The casket industry has tried to prevent the technology from being legalized in a number of jurisdictions.

Although the Roman Catholic Church has joined other religious lobbyists in opposing legalization of alkaline hydrolysis in at least four states, there's a lack of broad consensus on the issue among Catholics, as evidenced by Bishop Tutu's choice.

The state Catholic conference opposed New York's attempt to legalize the process in 2012 on grounds of church doctrine: "The Church's reverence for the sacredness of the human body and its dignity arises out of concern for both the body's natural and supernatural properties," it said. "Processes involving chemical digestion of human remains do not sufficiently respect this dignity." The Catholic Conference also voiced concerns that the bill could lead to individuals being "bio-cremated" against their will.

Some believe the conference will eventually reverse its position, as the church did with cremation. Sister Renée Mirkes, PhD, of the Franciscan Sisters of Christian Charity and director of the influential Center for NaProEthics, made an argument for the scientific advantages of the process in the *National Catholic Bioethics Quarterly* in 2008. "The Catholic Church has sound theological reasons for its unswerving promotion of burial as the normative practice for bodily disposition," she wrote. But "given its environmental, geographical and public health advantages, predictions are that requests for alkaline hydrolysis, once the process is legalized, will rival and perhaps exceed current US requests for cremation." When considering the choice of alkaline hydrolysis, she continued, one must consider whether it would "qualify 'in cases of necessity' as a moral alternative to Christian burial?" Her conclusion: "The process of alkaline hydrolysis is, in and of itself, a morally neutral action. When chosen for serious reasons, that is, out of necessity and in a way that confesses belief in the resurrection of the body, alkaline hydrolysis is a moral means of final bodily disposition."

Many Catholics, concerned about the impact of cremation on the global environment, believe a serious, necessary reason to use alkaline hydrolysis already exists, and that this will only become more apparent as the number of bodies requiring disposal climbs annually. Virginia Polytechnic Institute professor Philip Olson realizes there is opposition to the process but says many people find it "perfectly acceptable, if not preferable" to the alternatives, and that many Catholics are accepting the science and benefits of alkaline hydrolysis. "Some people will pay more for [it]," he says. "They think it's worth spending more to do something that's environmentally friendly."

There is still another form of opposition to alkaline hydrolysis. This is the "ick factor." Some people, says CANA's Kemmis, think "it's gross to dissolve bodies in acid and disrespectful to 'flush grandma down the drain'." Their misgivings aren't based on fact, she says. Alkaline hydrolysis doesn't use acids and the wastewater does not contain "bits of grandma, especially compared to the wastes of embalming."

Those who favour the process say it's no more repulsive or disrespectful than any other form of disposition, including cremation. Josh Slocum of the Funeral Consumers Alliance says there's nothing particularly distasteful about alkaline hydrolysis, although he acknowledged in his 2011 book *Final Rights* that "few of us would want to open the canister and watch." On the other hand, few would want to look inside a furnace when cremation is taking place.

Bioengineer Troy Hottle says cremation isn't necessarily something one wants to think about. For example, after the fire, comes the hammer. The brain is well protected by the skull, a large strong bone that sometimes must be smashed before the cremulator, or grinder, can reduce it to fragments.

The "ick factor" is often played up by opponents of legalization at the state level, something that clearly irritates Slocum: "Finding alkaline hydrolysis 'icky' has not a goddamned thing to do with whether it should be legal or not. Effluent from the process discharged into sewers has no bearing on the issue. Funeral homes for years have been flushing all the blood, body fluids, formaldehyde and formalin solutions into the sewers, yet have never been required to have a special license."

Despite the regulatory, religious, and cultural opposition, alkaline hydrolysis is here to stay as an alternative form of human disposition. It's a proven technology. It took a hundred years for traditional cremation to reach 5 percent of dispositions in the United States, notes Kemmis, who believes that alkaline hydrolysis businesses will find success on a much shorter timeline. What's needed, she says, is improved public education and enough regulatory stability for funeral businesses to feel comfortable making the leap into this new technology.

Whether they use high-temp or low-temp machines, advocates of alkaline hydrolysis agree that it is an answer to the looming crisis over disposition of bodies, and a preferable one to conventional cremation and ground burial. "It's one answer," Sullivan says. "I don't think it's going to be the be-all

and end-all or a panacea to all the issues with flame cremation. But, like alternative energy and others, composting and
other ones that I don't even see on the horizon, it's all good.
The more the merrier and that means there's a quicker move
away from flame cremation."

Adds Sullivan's rival, Joe Wilson: "With all the deaths that
are going to face our planet every day going forward, all the
techniques better be considered and put into practice before
the system gets overwhelmed."

Funeral director Drew Gray says people he meets are
asking why we incinerate anymore. "We're all looking for
alternatives," he says. "And aquamation has a certain taste-
fulness factor. We have to make death as palatable as we can."

CHAPTER SEVEN

The mushroom solution

*"Earth knows no desolation. She smells regeneration in the
moist breath of decay."*

—George Meredith

Mycelium (or mushroom) coffins are not the first technology
to be called the new normal in funerals. But, along with other
new approaches to disposing of bodies in the greenest-pos-
sible ways, using mycelium, or mushroom fibre, is showing
promising signs of–literally–taking root.

"That's definitely what we're aiming for–it's how nature
does it," bio-designer and architect Bob Hendrikx, said in an
interview from his Loop Biotech company headquarters in
Delft, the Netherlands. The way it's been done for too many
years, he said, preparing a person's body for disposition by
cutting down a beautiful tree for a coffin, putting the body in a

concrete box "and letting it rot for ten or twenty years doesn't make a lot of sense."

Hendrikx was a twenty-five-year-old undergraduate in bio-design architecture at the Delft University of Technology when he first developed the concept of placing human bodies in a mushroom coffin, resting on a cushion of fungi. The first disposition of a human body with his rapidly composting "living coffin" took place in late 2020. The coffin, which looks a bit like Styrofoam, is made from mycelium, a root-like structure of fungus found in and on soil and many other substances. Mycelium is "nature's recycler," says Hendrikx. While traditional methods pollute the soil, "for us, it was a no-brainer, and the cool thing about it is that the process can actually be much cheaper than producing a (regular) coffin." There is no wood or metal in mushroom coffins, although wood chips are included as food for mycelium.

Hendrikx founded, owns, and manages Loop Biotech. As of late 2021, he had delivered living cocoons to six countries: the Netherlands, Belgium, Germany, Austria, the United Kingdom, and the United States. The company has expanded its Netherlands-based production facility to 1,200 square-metres, turning out 100 mycelium-based mushroom coffins a month. But that's just a start. It now employs a staff of over 100 and has had coverage from CNN, European magazines, and business media. Hendrikx points out that the company's facility is huge, "but looking at the market, it's really small."

Loop Biotech's 2022 price per coffin, excluding shipping costs, is competitive with most other disposition methods, including cremation and alkaline hydrolysis. The mushroom coffins can be ordered online at a total price of €1,495 ($1,631/$2,079 CAD), and with a discounted buy-now-pay-later voucher for €1,250 ($1,364/$1,738 CAD) as potential customers anticipate their future passing.

Decomposition of a body using a traditional method, by casket burial or the green burial process, can take at least a decade, and much longer in a thick casket with varnished wood and metals. The mycelium coffin, while still requiring burial space, is absorbed into soil in a month to forty-five days, and the body it contains within two to three years. The body meets the natural environment much faster than in a conventional coffin and the mycelium and microorganisms within the moss accelerate the decomposition process. "Therefore the body degrades faster," he says.

Hendrikz Hendrikx, who worked in his twenties as a research associate at MIT, obtained initial seed funding from two large Dutch funeral cooperatives, CUVO and De Laatste Eer, both of which believe in his concept. He's appreciative of the angel investments but he's on the hunt for more. "We're focusing on getting large investments on board and really making this happen," he says. "We're going into the process of who fits our profile best and who gives the best deal."

Loop Biotech received the 2021 ASN Bank Award, a Dutch prize for sustainable start-ups that "make the world a little greener." By September of that year, after its expansion, it had a stock of hand-made "living cocoons" ready for use. It can deliver them within a day to locations in the Netherlands, Belgium, and Germany. The company invites inquiries and orders from funeral directors everywhere through its website at loop-biotech.com. Its free Discovery Box contains everything needed to understand the technology, including a piece of the mycelium material.

Not only is his technology eco-friendly, Hendrikx says, "we actually have a positive environmental impact, because what we do is recover the polluted soil that's in ground from decades of wrong burial and chemicals in our bodies." "The cool thing," he explains, "is that mycelium has the ability to neutralize the toxins from the body and the soil and turn it into nutrients that new plants can absorb and thereby increase biodiversity."

Mycelium was used at Chernobyl to start cleaning the soil after the 1986 disaster there. A lot of government industrial sites also clean their soil with mycelium, an organism that lives everywhere in the world, even in deserts. "So it's actually fortifying the soil, instead of polluting it," says Hendrikx. "That's the biggest change we're making." Ninety-two percent of all plant species rely on mycelium to survive, he adds. It is the biggest recycler on earth.

Interest from the funeral industry has been generally supportive. "A lot of people wish to collaborate," says Hendrikx. "It's important to keep in mind that [the funeral industry] is one of the most conservative and slow industries to adapt. But some companies have really proved to me that they want to change, [even if] they do it for marketing purposes . . . if you know what I mean." It helps that the mushroom coffins don't require huge investments in new equipment or processes and can be accommodated within the existing burial system.

CUVO and De Laatste Laatse Eer cooperatives helped fund Loop Biotech. Its director, Franks Franse, says that as a regional funeral organization, it's important for it to be involved in this kind of sustainable innovation: "It fits our objective to be a sustainable co-operative funeral service." Ed Bixby, president of the US Green Burial Council, says he's "impressed with the innovative concept" and is keen to learn more. "The cost," he says, "does seem most appropriate and not terribly expensive in any way, but in comparison to conventional (methods) very affordable."

Anita van Loon, director of Uitvaartstichting Hilversum, which operates three cemeteries overlooking hiking trails and forests in northern Holland, believes now is the moment for these kinds of developments. People are looking for a cleaner society and new and more natural funerals. "Loop Biotech fits so well," she says. "We give the body back to nature." The more religious may hesitate, van Loon says, but with young adults, "there will be a new generation interested in this new method. All the effort we've put into a cleaner way of living fits well with the natural way of dying."

Evert de Niet, chair of GreenLeave, a Dutch consortium of funeral organizations, calls the Loop Biotech process "promising" and "a strong concept." "It might be an eye-opener to governments," de Niet suggests, "to keep in mind regarding the law and regulations in relation to forms of funeral services."

Another eco-friendly feature of Loop Biotech products is their use of local materials. The mycelium and raw materials all come from the Netherlands. "Most large coffin manufacturers in the Netherlands import their wood from eastern Europe and call it sustainable," says Hendrikx. "Our vision is to enrich the world and save the natural world. That's the only reason we exist."

One challenge Loop company may face, as with any ground burial, is the growing scarcity and increased costs of cemetery land. But the mycelium coffins are gone in less than two months and the bodies are returned to the earth within three years.

Loop plans to set up additional local factories that work with the local mycelium species and raw materials. With its moulding system, it can grow 200 coffins per year. The mycelium-growing production process doesn't require heat, light, or electricity. Nature does all the work, Hendrkx explains.

Can his company keep pace with the massive mortality increases forecast for baby-boomers around the world? "The key is upscaling our facilities and production because we know people want it," says Hendrikx. "The answer is, we have to." To that end, Loop Biotech is already working with the largest coffin manufacturer in the Netherlands. "If that deal works, then we can go really big," says Hendrikx. His long-term goal is to ink similar deals with casket manufacturers in other countries.

CHAPTER EIGHT

Composting isn't just for food waste

"Death is like mud. It's dirty, messy, and incredibly tough to walk through, but surprisingly, it holds vital ingredients to life, and when seeds are planted, it can help sprout new life."
—Caleb Wilde in *Confessions of a Funeral Director* (2017).

Wilde's statement is especially appropriate to a relatively new disposition technique for human bodies known as composting, or natural organ reduction (NOR). It's not unrelated to conventional burial, which through natural processes reduces a body to its most basic elements. The objective of composting is also to return the body to earth by natural methods, only speeding it up a bit.

At least five companies are now offering composting of human bodies. Three are in Washington state, where the legislature approved the method in 2019. A Jewish funeral home in Colorado offers composting, and the process also has been legalized in Oregon. It was also legalized in California in September 2022 (taking effect in 2027) over opposition from the state's Catholic Conference. (The process was initially legalized in 2017 for use by the medical school anatomy lab at the University of California.)

Katrina Spade, a forty-two-year-old architectural designer, founded her Seattle-based company, Recompose, in 2017, although the concept originated years earlier. Billing itself as the world's first human composting facility, it has a decidedly progressive outlook, drawing on "queer feminist practices of inclusion and equity," and "committed to advocating and protecting for the rights of BIPOC (black, indigenous and people of colour), religious minorities, and undocumented people."

Spade says her company is part of the death-care "revolution" in which bodies are placed in a reusable vessel with carbon-rich natural materials like wood chips and alfalfa and straw, combined with oxygen to increase microbial activity. This pile, as the *New York Times* describes the process, will start "cooking. Bacteria release enzymes that break down tissue into component parts like amino acids, and eventually, the nitrogen-rich molecules bind with the carbon-rich ones, creating a soil-like substance. Temperatures reach around 140 degrees, often higher, and the heat kills common pathogens. Done correctly, there should be no smell."

The 131°F (55°C) heat generated by composting destroys most disease-causing pathogens. But, as with cremation and low-temperature alkaline hydrolysis, people who have died as a result of diseases such as Creutzfeldt-Jakob, are not eligible for composting.

After about a month, the remains from composting are reduced to approximately one cubic yard of soil. These remains are given to the deceased person's family, in the same manner as remains from cremation, or to conservation groups that use them to rehabilitate forests. "Composting makes people think of banana peels and coffee grounds," says Spade. "[But] our bodies have nutrients. What if we could grow new life after we've died?"

Composting human bodies is based on sound technology, says Chandler Cummins, development manager at Advanced Composting Technologies in Candler, North Carolina, who's worked in the field for fifteen years. "Composting is what nature wants to do," he says. "It wants to create living beings and then breaks down those beings when they're no longer living. It's just a different type of composting. It lets thermo-dynamics take over." Cummins adds, "It's all about controls. You want to speed up what nature can do. The better the diet, the better the microbes are going to be and you try to make them as happy as you can."

Dr. Troy Hottle, senior analyst with Eastern Research and an early consultant and advisor on Katrina Spade's project, says that as opposed to ground burial and cremation, composting not only avoids the burden of CO_2, it advances the sequestering of carbon, reducing its release into the atmosphere. (He also recommends planting trees to further reduce the number of harmful particulates.) Less carbon in the atmosphere will reduce greenhouse gases and the impacts of climate change, he explains, estimating that the total carbon savings resulting from composting is about the equivalent of what's absorbed in one year by an acre of forest.

As of July 2022, Recompose charges $7,000 for disposition of a body, all costs included. The price covers transportation of the body from locations within Washington State. Outside the state, the transportation cost is based on proximity to the Recompose location. (A pre-payment plan can be arranged.) By May 2021, it had reduced forty human bodies to soil and Spade said at the time that more than 700 people had chosen to use the Recompose technology.

In the wake of an initial flurry of media attention, Recompose was proposing to expand rapidly and build an 18,500-square-foot "greenhouse design" to operate in. It has since scaled back operations and revised its plans. In March 2022, Spade reported the company had raised $9 million of its $10 million capitalization goal to fund future growth. Its investors are not big-time venture capitalists but individuals, families, and organizations putting up between $100,000 and $250,000. The company has tentative plans to open a second operation in Seattle. Its attempt to launch an operation in California hit a snag in mid-2021 when the state legislature vetoed the technology.

Doubts have been raised about the viability and marketability of human composting.

The California-based Green Burial Council will not endorse Recompose, because of its refusal to share information about its technology. The council was primarily troubled by Recompose's "lack of transparency and accountability," says the council's president, Ed Bixby. "I think there's a lot of smoke and mirrors there."

Bixby is also sceptical about the demand for human composting. "I don't see a large market for this, at least not at this point in time," he says. "They're going to service people who want it, but in my opinion, they're going to make a very small impact. I don't see people choosing this solution."

The composting process isn't gentle, says Bixby, contrary to how it's described. There's no mention of the bones and teeth having to be ground up following reduction of the body to soil. "The gruesome details will be too much to bear for the grieving families," he says. Organic reduction requires a lot of turbulence and moving parts that aren't so gentle, he explained. "Quite honestly (it) can be quite a brutal process. It's not like laying someone down on a bed of roses and having them disappear. I can't believe that you put grandma in a pile of mulch and a month later she's topsoil."

Herland Forest Cemetery in Washington State uses similar methods, turning a body mixed with wood chips, moisture, and oxygen, plus added bacteria, protozoa, and fungi, into compost. Its process operates off the power grid, using photo-voltaic panels to supplement the heat in its chambers. Herland also offers full-body burial, plus ash burial, ash scattering, and living-tree memorials. The price for composting is $3,000, dropping to $2,700 if the family is directly involved. (The state requires a family member or an embalmer to lay the body to rest in an organic reduction cradle. The family's involvement saves the embalming fee.) Walt Patrick, stewardship manager at Herland Forest, says the community-based, not-for-profit cemetery was the state's first facility to offer natural organic reduction for human bodies, and the first licensed operator for the procedure in the United States.

The third composting venture in Washington, Return Home, operates an 11,500-square-foot facility. Founder Micah Truman's trademarked "Terramation" process transforms the body into soil by similar methods. By September 2021, Truman had "recomposed" sixteen bodies in a sixty-day period. His facility is located in Auburn, a Seattle suburb, and charges $4,950 per body. Truman, whose background is finance, intends to offer the natural organ reduction service directly to consumers and also as a trade service, working with existing funeral homes, which will charge their own fees.

In Colorado, Seth Viddal, with coaching from Herland's Walt Patrick, wasted no time building a composting vessel in a Denver warehouse shortly after the state legalized the process. Viddal employs a seven-by-three-foot wooden box, with wheels that allow it to be moved around, providing agitation and oxygen, helping the body achieve compost. He charges $7,900 per body, almost four times the cost of flame cremation.

The concept of natural organ reduction of humans is new, but some in the death-care field are already expressing doubts about its future. The relatively high cost is seen as a problem that may limit it to a niche market. Death-care consultant Shane Neufeld ventures that if the new method is ever going to hit the mainstream, it will require a lot of investment. Unless there is evidence that the method is going to be popular enough to gain market share from cemeteries and cremation, investors won't invest. "If I were speculating, I don't anticipate it's going to become terribly popular."

Of the three composting projects in the Washington State, Bixby believes Herland Forest's concept is the best and most viable, albeit on a modest scale. Walt Patrick at Herland, he says, has been forthright and talked to the council about its work. He enlightened the council about the process, which up to that point was unclear. Patrick had thirty years' experience composting large farm animals before he advanced into the disposition of human bodies.

Herland Forest operates as a not-for-profit and has no investors to keep happy. "We're not having to rush things in order to generate revenue to pay dividends to stockholders," Patrick says. "We're a non-profit with a paid-for facility . . . We don't feel we need to accelerate the process by grinding up the cadaver. We're committed to allowing the process to proceed at its own pace." As with both cremation and aquamation, Herland Forest will pulverize the bones after an extended period of decomposition. A camera goes into the chamber to inspect the remains so the body's state of decomposition won't be a matter of guesswork.

Patrick apparently offered his time and advice to Spade at Recompose but was turned down. "That's unfortunate for them," says Bixby, "because he might have helped [Recompose]. Now if someone were to call us and ask about this, we can't recommend them. It's buyer beware." He loves the "blue-sky" thinking but worries companies like Recompose will be unable to produce enough revenue to service their debt and end up becoming a black eye for innovation in the funeral industry. He "certainly would not invest" in the company or its products.

Troy Hottle, formerly with the US Environmental Protection Agency, defends Recompose against media articles that disparage composting "as a grotesque way of treating bodies." They don't understand what happens to the compost, he says. Some erroneously suggest it will be made available commercially, with people spreading it on their lawns without realizing it.

Instead, he says, it provides a mechanism to dispose of a body respectfully, with no carbon footprint. "The biomass of the body itself is retained in the soil," he says. "The green burial folks will likely see it as sort of hand-in-hand to their approach as a low-energy way without necessitating land use."

Hottle also has a response to Christian groups that consider composting an outrage, a desecration that destroys the body. Some cremation processes can be "pretty gruesome" as well, he says, if anyone bothered to contemplate what's involved, which they should before making a final decision. "If people knew that, while you're getting burned, there's somebody or a machine poking your body so that it breaks up–if more of that was understood by the public–they'd have a much better appreciation of how non-invasive composting is, compared to traditional methods." People also need to understand the embalming process or what happens to the body inside a casket that's *not* exposed to the soil and elements, he adds.

It's important, says Hottle, to understand how science copes with a growing population and the level of mortality that goes with it. He doesn't necessarily see composting as the sole answer to the coming crisis, with millions of deaths of baby boomers forecast over the next few decades. "I don't know if there's any one answer," he says. "I don't think we can take all the options off the table. Creating more environmentally-friendly options will enable people to make choices in line with what (they) prefer to happen to their body. The more people there are, the more significant any impacts associated with deaths will be."

Human composting is still in its infancy and not widely available. Josh Slocum of the Funeral Consumers Alliance, noting Recompose's $7,000 fee, thinks the price point has to change if it's ever going to be a viable option for most. "Families who need to spend less are going to go for what's affordable, whatever the technology may be," he says. Options like human composting are generally only practical for people who "have the disposable income and inclination to do so," unless the companies' volumes can moderate their costs.

Chandler Cummins agrees that price is a problem but thinks scale might change that: "You can sell what the market can bear and people want alternatives, but you can also over price yourself and never get a sale. If they're only going to get a hundred or so people a year, they're going to have to charge one thing. If they're going to get ten thousand people, they can charge something else."

CHAPTER NINE

Outlier methods, from reef burials to SpaceX

"I don't think we can take all the options off the table. Creating more environmentally-friendly options will enable people to make choices."

—Troy Hottle

With mortality numbers growing and casket burials and cremation increasingly seen as distasteful, costly, and environmentally unfriendly, the search for alternative methods of human disposal continues. Some new options are more palatable, affordable, and comforting than others. Some are unproven and may turn out to be dead ends. A number considered below are extravagant, and it should be noted that spending on the disposition of a person's body is no guarantee of satisfaction. People often think how much they pay demonstrates how much their family member was loved. But spending more than the family can afford is a pointless way of dealing with loss or the feeling of not having done more while the loved one lived. Nonetheless, some of the methods that follow are quite valid and do provide varying degrees of satisfaction.

Reef burials

Memorial or eternal reefs involve artificially constructed marine habitats. The cremated bodies of people seeking green burial options can be laid to rest as a part of these artificial reefs, becoming a habitat for marine life. A unique form of memorialization, reef balls will be of special interest to ocean lovers concerned with the marine environment.

In areas where coral reefs have been destroyed, artificial structures like reef balls have been used for years to repair damage. Enduring artificial reefs are considered a useful method to restore reef systems to a natural and productive balance. Memorial reef balls, made with the addition of remains from the dead, are a newer invention. But there are already thousands of memorial reef balls sunk off the eastern seaboard of the United States and elsewhere. They can be dedicated with or without the family present.

The cremated remains of families' loved ones are incorporated into a special mixture of neutralized, environmentally safe, marine-grade concrete. Each formed ball or "pearl" is hollow and perforated with several holes for marine life to swim through. They can weigh up to five tons. Families may insert messages and items reminding them of the deceased relative, provided they're not harmful to the environment or to marine life. They can then take the completed reef ball out to sea, say a few words and (with help) drop it overboard. Loved ones are provided with GPS coordinates of the resting place so they can dive or sail to visit the remains.

Large reef memorials can accommodate multiple sets of remains, so families can be included and placed together. Memorial plaques may be installed with the person's name, date of birth, and date of death.

Eternal reef structures are provided by companies and sited in designated memorial reef areas. There are more than thirty permitted locations for reef memorials in the United States, including off the coasts of Florida, New Jersey, and Texas. Neptune Memorial Reef is an underwater columbarium off the south Florida coast. It has become a final resting place for more than 6,000 people. The reef, forty feet below the surface, is visited by 2,000 divers each month. In the United Kingdom, where the Crown Estate owns the seabed, they are located in a square-kilometre site off the southern coast.

Costs can vary, depending on which organization is chosen to select the site, construct the reef, and determine the size and shape of the memorial. Depending on how large the reef ball is, costs range from $4,000 to $7,500.

At present, few countries have policies in place that cover sea burials of cremated remains specifically, although most governments permit bodies to be disposed of at sea. The latter is, of course, a long-standing disposition option for ocean lovers. The body, suitably prepared and weighted, is dropped into the sea from a ship or plane.

Promession

This technology is so new it does not yet exist for human use. Intended for disposition of bodies in an eco-friendly way, promession initially received extensive media attention in 2001. Invented by the late Susanne Wiigh-Mäsak, a Swedish biologist, it had been in development stages for almost twenty years. But it's had a long, complicated, and troubled history. Although Wiigh-Mäsak died in 2020, her project is still seeking advocates and investors.

Wiigh-Mäsak disliked the term "disposition." She preferred to call it "caretaking." Her company, Promessa Organic AB, promised to "take care of the body to support new life." The process involves freeze-drying human bodies in liquid nitrogen and then using a "cyrogenic vibration module" to crush them to powder. The crumbled remains are then placed in a chamber where 70 percent of the water content is removed, reducing its weight. Metals, including fillings or artificial hips, are removed by magnetism or with sieves. The dry powder is next placed in a biodegradable-casket and is buried in top soil, where aerobic bacteria break down the remains into humus in less than a year. The technology so far has been used only on the bodies of pigs, anatomically similar to humans, although with thicker skins and more fat.

The first promession equipment, called a "promoter," was intended to be launched in 2005. Twelve dead bodies were then kept frozen, pending the equipment's availability.

The head of the Swedish Funeral Directors Associations, Ulf Lernéus, says the Church of Sweden initially claimed that freeze-drying bodies would be covered by existing laws governing cremation. The claim helped raise capital for the concept. But then Swedish legal authorities stepped in, Lernéus says, requesting "more facts and fewer mantras." By 2006, the Swedish Tax Agency had announced that the method would not be a reality in the foreseeable future. Authorities eventually demanded that the frozen bodies be buried.

"One can ignore all the nice talk and all the betrayed promises about freeze drying," Lernéus says, "if it weren't for all these deceased people who had been frozen for almost fourteen years." The patent, he adds, was sold to English interests in 2017, but little has been heard since. "The most impressive thing in this story is how Susanne Wiigh-Mäsak was able to market something that did not exist for a very long time," Lernéus says. "Even today, there are lot of people in Sweden who believe the method still exists."

Not everyone is sceptical. A Kansas lobbyist for Sierra Club, Zack Pistora, was quoted in 2019 as saying, "newer, greener methods of burial, like promession, may conserve resources and cause less pollution." The quote is accurate, Pistora says, but the operative word is "may." He can't openly endorse promession, "because I don't know enough about it."

Lisa Carlson, director of the Funeral Ethics Organization (and former head of the Funeral Consumers Alliance), still considers promession "a great idea." But her successor at FCA, John Slocum, calls it "a gimmick, a Rube Goldberg contraption." Swedish anatomy professor Bengt Johansson is even less diplomatic, condemning the technology as "completely unproven." The human body, he says, can't be disintegrated by slight shaking, even after being frozen in liquid nitrogen. It would be like trying to shake apart a frozen roast of lamb.

The inventor's husband and now Promessa's CEO, Peter Mäsak, insists that while the promession project is currently inactive, research is ongoing. The company has been working with an engineer to build what he says is an innovative "cyrovibration" model. Promessa supporters are looking for new representatives or "ambassadors" around the world as well as investors. He insisted that all kinds of obstacles have been overcome thanks to a solid business strategy "that places ethics and sustainability at the core of our company."

Burial pods

Another method still in the idea stage is Capsula Mundi ("world's capsule" in Latin), an organic egg-shaped pod designed by two Italian artists. Anna Vitelli and Raoul Bretzel say the pods would contain a tree or seed, fertilized by a decomposing body in a foetal position and planted in a forested area. The pod allows a body to add to the soil's nutrients and become part of the natural landscape.

Capsula Mundi's pods, first shown at an exhibition in Milan in 2019, attracted significant attention, mainly from the younger generations, for their sleek design and gentle environmental approach. "Capsula Mundi wants to emphasize that we are part of nature's cycle of transformation," its developers told *Dezeen*, an architectural magazine.

So far, however, Capsula Mundi is marketing only biodegradable urns to be used for ashes (cremains). The human burial pod, says artist Citelli, "is not yet ready for the market." Or, perhaps, vice versa.

Bodies in orbit

SpaceX rockets now launch human remains, or a portion of them, into orbit. Funeral flights, organized by the company Celesta, cost upwards of $5,000 to fly one gram of "participant" remains into orbit, reports *Business Insider*. Since its 1994 founding, Celesta has flown cremated remains on fifteen different rockets into sub-orbital flights and six into earth Earth's orbit.

There are different different-sized capsules on offer. They hold varying amounts of the remains of one or more participants. Two NASA astronauts (or a portion of them) have departed the earth this way, as did *Star Trek* actor James "Scotty" Doohan in 2008. (His co-star William Shatner, who's already had one real-life space adventure, plans to be buried under a redwood on land he owns in northern California.) Astrogeologist Eugene Shoemaker is, to date, the only person buried on the moon. His remains were taken there in 1998 by a NASA probe.

Elysium is another space-burial company, founded in 2013. It offers a "lunar memorial service" for around $10,000. That involves delivering small portions of the deceased human remains to the moon. The Elysium Star space mausoleum satellites are designed to remain in space for two years. For those concerned about littering the ionosphere with the cremated remains of dead humans, Elysium says the ashes would theoretically decay in orbit and return to Earth as a shooting star.

Sky burial

Also called "bird-scattered," "excarnation," or "celestial burial," sky burial is a funeral practice in which a human body is placed on a mountaintop or tower to decompose while exposed to the elements or eaten by scavenging animals, mainly carrion birds.

It is still the method of choice by Parsis, an ethnoreligious group in India. Bodies are left in what's called "the tower of silence." In Buddhist teaching, the locations are known as charnel grounds. Some Tibetans and Mongols, who adhere to Buddhism, teach transmigration and see no need to preserve the body, as it's considered an empty vessel. Tibetans believe that there is a great honour knowing that a human body will go back to nature, nourishing nature's creatures, usually bearded vultures, or Dakinis, meaning sky dancers, the Tibetan equivalent of angels. Sky burial is a fading tradition. Few such places remain in operation today as society has become more urbanized and religion marginalized. Cremation has replaced sky burial in many countries.

Mushroom suit

In a variation on mycelium-based interment, artist Jae Rhim Lee has developed an "infinity burial suit" that involves flesh-eating mushrooms purportedly breaking down human bodies, cleansing them of toxins, and returning the remains to soil.

An artist in her forties, Lee was born in South Korea but grew up in Georgia and studied at MIT. She says the goal of her California company, Coeio, is to offer a new way of thinking about death. Her TED talk on the subject drew 1.2 million views on YouTube. Her technology, however, has been called into question.

The burial suit–or mushroom death suit–is impregnated with a mix of mushroom (mycelium) spores and other micro-organisms. But informed critics say it differs little from normal body disposition and simply won't work. Among the doubters is the US Green Burial Council, which cites "concerns in the conservation community regarding necessity, viability, and scientific support" of the mushroom suit theory. It says the method is "not in concert with the GBC's commitment to natural, unfettered, and unimpeded decomposition."

In January 2015, a sixty-four-year-old carpenter with a terminal disease wrote Lee's company to say his time was running out. He wanted a mushroom suit and became the method's first customer. Four years later, actor Luke Perry (best known for his work on the TV series *Beverly Hills, 90210*), died of a massive stroke and was buried in a mushroom suit. Coeio, at last report, was still taking orders online for the suit, priced at around $1,500.

Body farms

Body farms are research facilities where decomposition can be studied, particularly for forensic purposes. They were conceived in 1987 by anthropologist William Bass, an anatomical researcher and forensic anthropologist who began studying the processes and timetables involved in human body decay at the University of Tennessee. Individuals agree to have their remains used for this purpose. Their bodies are placed outside in the elements to give researchers the opportunity to study natural decomposition. Some see this is as distasteful; advocates stress that researchers show respect for the donated bodies.

The work done at these farms has done more than boost our understanding of decomposition. There are applications in anthropology, forensic science, law enforcement, and related disciplines. Many investigators use body farms in criminal cases, as well as deaths by fire, drowning, or other causes. They have fostered the development of techniques to glean information from human remains, such as the timing and circumstances of death.

Seven such facilities exist across the United States, from Florida to Northern Michigan. One operated by Texas State University covers twenty-six acres. Similar ones operate in Australia and Canada, the most recent in the province of Quebec.

Bass's original farm was established on a three-acre site near Knoxville. He retired in his seventies, but is still an active researcher at age ninety-three. He is known for investigating The Tri-State Crematory Scandal in 2002, where nearly 350 non-cremated bodies had been dumped in northwest Georgia. He's also remembered for performing the autopsy on the exhumed remains of singer-songwriter J. P. ("The Big Bopper") Richardson, killed in a 1959 plane crash with pop musicians Buddy Holly and Richie Valens. He makes no apology for the work he has performed, although, he says, "You've got to laugh to keep your sanity."

CHAPTER TEN

Body donation, "the kindest gift"

"Mortui Prosumus Vitae"
—("Even in death do we serve life") inscription
over a communal grave for body donors at
Bremgarten cemetery, Bern, Switzerland.

It has been called "the last, best thing people can do." The donation of human bodies for research is regarded by the medical community as the greatest gift anyone can make. Individuals and families are encouraged to consider full body donation as the most compassionate alternative to conventional burial when the time comes for this crucial decision, at or before the time of death.

In most countries, body donations must follow state, provincial, or local laws. (Donors should also be aware that the process of donation varies from state to state.) A medical institution may have additional requirements, but can't have fewer than those dictated by law. Consent for donation is provided by completing forms for the purpose available from any school of anatomy, or orally in the presence of witnesses prior to death. Usually, one must register with the closest university medical school's "anatomical gift" program. In the United States, close to 20,000 bodies a year are donated this way. Donation forms can vary among institutions. The next of kin may also give consent after death.

Donors and their families have long been encouraged to contribute their bodies to anatomy laboratories to advance medical and scientific knowledge through willed body programs. In the strictest sense, however, it's not considered disposition. Donated bodies are not used indefinitely.

The gifting of bodies to legitimate medical science has obvious value. The study of the human body is one of the first and most important courses in the education of physicians. The study of anatomy serves as the foundation for training in surgery, pathology, and physiology. Surgeons often practice clinical procedures on human cadavers. The donations also benefit kinesiology students, physical and occupational therapists, and even engineers. Many anatomy schools include dentistry students. Bodies are also useful to researchers in pursuit of medical advances that will impact current and future generations.

The need for specimens at university medical schools has remained consistent for years, says Dr. Ann Zumwalt, associate professor of anatomy at Boston University. "There's an amazing payoff for the students who have gone through the anatomy lab experience," she says. "The payoff to both students and to society is enormous."

Bodies for study and research are fixed, or prepared and embalmed with formalin. Some schools use other techniques to maintain a body's lifelike qualities. Physical fixation can be performed by freeze drying, although many schools don't use that method. Plastination is another process used in anatomy to preserve bodies or body parts, making it possible for students to conduct dissections without the odour of formalin. A plastinated cadaver also feels like a living body because specimen integrity is maintained. At some labs, a latex material may be injected into the vascular system to help identify veins and arteries by colour, though not all medical schools do this.

For students of anatomy, recent donations of new technology have been invaluable. Ultrasound for clinical imaging, and monitors and cameras, now allow entire classes to simultaneously visualize the anatomical structures of living subjects or of donors. New virtual dissection tables, called "anatomages," let students view the body without chemicals and smells from cadavers. "It's the most advanced 3D visualization system for anatomy and physiology being adopted in the world's leading medical schools," Zumwalt explains. "There are lots of things you can do with these tools."

There are differing views on whether full cadaver dissection should still be required for modern undergraduates. Some medical schools have abandoned costly dissection-based instruction in favour of alternatives, including prosection, medical imaging, living anatomy, and multimedia resources. And, as mentioned, programs in some countries have moved to virtual dissection entirely. But most anatomists agree that this method, which uses radiology images, can't substitute for the real thing. The decreased use of cadaver dissection can have a negative impact on students' anatomical knowledge.

Every donation is used to train as many people as possible, many of whom will go on to practice for three to four decades. "It's fundamental to what they do," says Dr. Edwin Moore, head of the University of British Columbia's anatomy school. "Every donation is going to impact the health and well-being of thousands of people in the coming years. It's important they know how valuable that donation was."

Universities, palliative care centres, and nursing homes reinforce the significance of body donor programs. Funeral homes also explain the option of donating bodies for teaching and research. And many physicians and nurses set examples by donating their bodies to anatomical research.

Zumwalt says that memorial ceremonies or "services of gratitude" are held annually at all anatomy schools to honour each year's donors and are attended by their family members. "We pay a lot of attention to the people who are the donors and their families," she stresses, "so we have a reputation that we care about people." Every medical school where she's worked is aware of this. They talk openly about gratitude for the donors and for the opportunity of conducting research thanks to their contribution. In the world of medical anatomy, she adds, it's the most important thing they talk about.

A donated body has to be approved by an ethics committee and students must adhere to a code of professionalism. "[Students] learn from the anatomy, but they also learn from the humanity of it," says Zumwalt. The procedure is obviously different from dissecting an animal, she explains. Students very much think about donors as once-living human beings, not mere specimens for study. "They're growing as future doctors and they're thinking about death and dying," she says, "they're thinking about who this person was, 'did they suffer in life and worry about the medical condition they had?'" It's sometimes hard cutting into that person, remembering their humanity, but the students also appreciate the need to "get the job done."

The supply of willed bodies in medical education and research has fortunately kept up with the increasing demand, although some schools have an easier time than others meeting the need for cadavers. Voluntary donations are more than enough for some, wrote Boston College law professor Ray Madoff in a 2009 paper. "This is particularly true for the most prestigious institutions, some of which have a surplus

of cadavers and thus have stringent requirements for donation." But lesser-known institutions often struggle to meet
their demand for bodies and that's where anatomy legislation helps to make more available, Madoff explained. The acts
apply to "unclaimed bodies," but rather than being directed at
the poor, they're more likely to apply to prisons and hospitals,
which would otherwise bury or cremate cadavers.

COVID-19 forced the Boston medical school to temporarily put its donation program on hold (it later re-opened).
Faculty has since been much more careful, Dr. Zumwalt says,
to ensure it doesn't accept a donor that has either contracted
COVID-19 or died from it. As a result, it can now accept fewer
donors resulting in less-than-ideal levels of supply. Dr. Bruce
Wainman, director of McMaster University's anatomy program in Hamilton, Ontario, also reports that COVID-19 has
had a negative impact on donations and acceptance.

The American Association for Anatomy (AAA), like other
responsible oversight organizations, stipulates that institutions should make all possible use of donation materials.
Shipment of cadavers should also follow government requirements. The body-broker sector, however, has frequently
managed to skirt those requirements, which often aren't
adequately enforced. More on this later.

There are also limitations on what donations anatomy
labs can accept. For example, anatomy schools cannot consider prospective donors who have died of a transmissible

disease. (Donated bodies are embalmed by the schools, which are naturally concerned about the health of their embalmers.) Ineligible for donation are bodies that have undergone recent surgery, with open incisions or unhealed scars, and the extremely overweight. Many labs don't accept donors under a certain age, though anatomy schools often accept donations from parents of very young children, even neonatal infants and stillborn foetuses. Medical schools are not inclined to accept a donated body if the immediate family withholds consent.

Bodies donated for medical research are not kept indefinitely. There's an ongoing debate about whether it's ethical to keep people's bodies beyond a certain time. McMaster's Dr. Wainman says how long a body is retained depends on what it's used for. If it's for a surgical skills course, it may be for weeks or months. If it's used for a dissection-based course, the process of embalming and leaving it fixed adds more time. However long they're kept, there must be a method for their disposition after they're studied for research. At the majority of medical schools, cremation is the norm and required by law.

At anatomy labs at the Mayo Clinic in Minnesota and universities in Florida, California, and Texas, however, the families of donor bodies can choose between alkaline hydrolysis and conventional cremation. "Some families want the body returned for earth burial," says Shaun Heath, the Mayo's former anatomical services director, "but that doesn't happen often."

The scope of the Mayo Clinic's work means people come there from all over the world and the contiguous United States for medical care. "They feel strongly about giving back for the care they've received here," Heath said. Eighty-six percent of Mayo donors are used for teaching procedural–or surgical–methods, with first-year students studying gross anatomy, and then in each of their four years of study.

Organ donation

As with donation of a human body to research and educa-tion, organ donation is a profoundly selfless act. The organ or tissue is removed in a sterile surgical procedure and transplanted into a recipient whose organ has failed or been damaged by disease or injury. A procurement organization determines the medical suitability of a donation based on the donor's medical history and age. The recipient will not know the donor's identity.

People of all ages should consider themselves potential donors as the need for organs is far greater than the number of donors. Families can also choose to donate a relative's body or organs. In most cases, donors can still have an open casket funeral. It is nevertheless important to discuss the impact of donating specific organs and tissues on the viewing with a recovery professional, who works with the funeral director to address such concerns.

Individuals who wish to be organ donors can join a donor registry providing legal consent for the anatomical gift of organs, tissue, and eyes (these choices are often included with your driver's license); register at any time by filling out a Document of Gift form; sign and carry an organ donor card; let family members and loved ones, a health-care provider, lawyer, or religious leader know of your wish to be a donor.

"The human body is the most complex system ever created," as business magnate and philanthropist Bill Gates has observed. "The more we learn about it, the more appreciation we have about what a rich system it is." Few acts contribute to that learning more than the donation of a body, in whole or in part, to medical science.

CHAPTER ELEVEN

The profits and scandals of body brokers

"There's a general idea in the United States that once you're dead, you're property. You have no more rights than an old refrigerator."
—Dr. Thomas Champney, University of Miami, Florida.

Donors beware.

The still-unregulated market for human bodies or body parts often borders on the obscene, reminiscent of nineteenth-century grave-robbing. The body trade ostensibly has developed in recent years to increase the availability of human cadavers for research. But operators sell cadavers, or parts of them, without the full knowledge or informed consent of donors. The activity of most of these brokers is clearly unethical and in some cases criminal. And the worst of the cases are stomach-turning.

An Arizona FBI raid in 2014 turned up one of the more grotesque instances of abuse (these stories seem mostly to emerge from the United States). The investigators found body parts in buckets and records of body sales to the defence department for use as crash test dummies. More than 140 body bags and more than 1,700 separate body parts were removed from the facility. There were buckets of heads, buckets or of arms, buckets of legs, and a cooler filled with male genitalia. The FBI raid was part of an investigation into the trafficking and sales of human body parts. Reuters News Agency reported that bodies appeared to have been dismembered with "a coarse instrument," a motorized saw, and that some body parts were sewn together in a "Frankenstein" manner.

Some investigating agents were treated for post-traumatic stress disorder. The outrage led to criminal charges and civil suits launched by families of the deceased that brought payouts of $58 million.

The actions of body-parts enterprises can be stomach-turning and devoid of any hint of respect for the dead. They work in a number of ways. Human tissue, body parts, and whole bodies have been known to be lifted from hospital morgues and funeral homes and sold to private research labs, multinational companies, or other profit-making industries. An entire human body can fetch as $10,000 on the black market.

People who have willed their bodies or organs to science and not been careful enough about who they dealt with often wind up not in the dignified environment of a teaching hospital or medical school but "in a row of trunks, limbless and headless, arrayed on gurneys in the ballroom of a resort hotel for a surgical training seminar," the *New York Times* reported.

For-profit transplant tissue banks are another problem. The American Association for Anatomy has called for a halt to their "unethical and criminal acts," which include giving misleading information to those interested in donating their bodies and to the families of the recently deceased, sometimes using bodies in illegal ways, and sometimes selling and storing them in illicit manners.

It is illegal to sell body parts in the United States, but there are no rules against charging for shipping and handling of body parts. "Delivery of an intact cadaver costs as little as $1,000," wrote the *Times*, "but different specialists seek out specific pieces of anatomy for their work, and individual parts can be expensive. A head can cost $500 in processing fees, according to brokers who handle such parts. A torso in good condition can fetch $5,000. A spine goes for as much as $3,500, a knee $650, a cornea $400. In 2002, a pharmaceutical company paid $4,000 for a box of fingernails and toenails.

The body trade ostensibly developed in recent years to increase the availability of human cadavers for research. But operators sell cadavers, or parts of them, without the full knowledge or informed consent of donors. The activity of most of these brokers is clearly unethical and in some cases criminal.

Body brokers will offer free cremation as an enticement to obtain bodies from families. In some cases, hospices have been referred to as "cash cows" because they harbour people nearing death who want a cheaper way to go. But they're also known to obtain bodies and cadaver parts against donor families' wishes from institutions which have a surplus.

In her 2006 book *Black Markets*, Michele Goodwin wrote that more than 200 private US companies treat and reprocess human body parts. One shouldn't assume that cadavers or parts donated to universities never go beyond those anatomy labs, she says. By-products of the procurement system take place in the shadow of the law. Skin, valves, brains, bones, and other human body parts are traded commercially between university hospitals, brokers, and biotech companies. It may not be wise, Goodwin cautioned, for donors to assume that bodies they donate for scientific purposes won't move from the institution into the stream of commerce.

Reuters reported in 2017 that body brokers received at least 50,000 bodies and distributed 182,000 body parts over a four-year period. The news agency also found that some funeral operators provide body brokers with access to potential donors, reaping finder's fees ranging over $1,400. Reuters highlighted an Oklahoma funeral home that, in 2009, invested

$650,000 for a 50 percent share of a Phoenix-based body broker, United Tissue Network. The body broker was forecasting $13.8 million in revenues for trade in 2,100 bodies over five years. One client company included human skulls, elbows, livers, and eyeballs in its inventory. In a five-year period, United Tissue sold close to 18,000 body parts to clients.

One thriving company, Science Care, founded by a Phoenix couple, turned the sale of donated bodies into $12.5 million windfall between 2012 and 2014, buying a custom-built plane and luxury homes from the proceeds before selling their shares to a private equity firm. Terms of the sale included written pledges from 100,000 people to donate their bodies to the company.

In 2012, an organization called Death Science arranged, for a paying audience, the public dissection of a ninety-eight-year-old war veteran's body in Portland, Oregon, calling it an educational display. The horrified widow of the deceased, who died of complications from COVID-19, called the dissection "horrible" and "unethical."

The UCLA suspended its Willed Body Program in 2004, and university police arrested its director, who was accused of trafficking in as many as 800 cadavers over six years. Another senior employee was also charged. The medical school's director said it was investigating the failure of its policies. It re-opened the program with more safeguards in 2005.

Probably the worst offender has been Biological Resource Center (BRC) in Arizona, the company which ran the "human chop shop" at the centre of the FBI raid mentioned above. Its owner, Stephen Gore, was accused of fraud and deception and ordered to pay $58 million in punitive and compensatory damages by a Maricopa County jury. Some of those bodies had been used for ballistics testing and in crash research.

Jim Stauffer of Arizona had donated the corpse of his seventy-five-year-old mother, Doris Stauffer, to BRC in 2014 expecting it to be used in Alzheimer's research. Instead, most of her body, including her brain, was sold to a US Army blast-testing research project. Her cadaver was belted into a chair beneath which an explosive device was detonated to give researchers "an idea of what the human body goes through when a vehicle is hit by an IED." Her son Jim, a plaintiff in the BRC civil action, had also, unknowingly, received back from BRC a container holding only the remains from one of his mother's hands, not her entire body.

Gwen Aloia, reported the *Daily Mail*, donated her husband's body to BRC, ostensibly for medical research, after he died of cancer. His body parts were found scattered over several different states and she still does not know if the ashes given to her by the company are indeed her husband's.

Federal authorities in 2011 caught a broker crossing into Canada with severed heads in a container also traced to BRC, Reuters reported. A year later, baggage handlers came across camper coolers containing severed heads in trash bags leaking blood at a warehouse in Detroit. A body broker supplied by BRC was convicted of selling and transporting infected body parts. In addition to the civil suits aimed at BRC, owner Stephen Gore was found guilty of operating an illegal business, sentenced to deferred jail time, plus probation, and forced to pay $121,000 in restitution.

Part of the problem is body brokers, unlike institutional medical schools, advertise aggressively, soliciting from hospices and nursing homes. "They really strongly advertise to get people to donate under false pretenses," says Dr. Thomas Champney of the University of Miami, Florida, one of the authors of a 2019 report from the National Library of Medicine that decried the "commercialization or commodification" of willed bodies in programs that generate profit. "They can make it sound very noble and altruistic to get donors, then chop them up and sell them for various prices." There are also well-known cases of kickbacks from funeral homes, he agrees. "There's lot of shady dealings in that regard." Anyone can start one of these body body-broker businesses without any formal training, certification, or state or federal licenses.

Medical school anatomy programs don't consider it ethical to advertise. "We don't think it's appropriate to go to hospitals and funeral homes and strong-arm people into donating bodies," says Champney. "We put ourselves at a disadvantage, but I think it's the right thing to do." More education of the general public is needed, he adds, to counter these companies' ability to prey on people's' ignorance.

Legitimate anatomy laboratories, most of them in medical schools, are disdainful of the largely profitable labs that obtain human cadavers from questionable sources for a range of costs. If a family is looking to save on funeral and cremation costs, they say, there are legitimate ways to donate a body without relying on body brokers. Reputable university medical programs can be trusted to provide respectful methods of disposition and a legitimate benefit to the science of medicine and the training of medical professionals. For-profit body brokers can be trusted only to look after their own bottom lines.

While reputable university programs are indeed mostly trustworthy, there have been painful exceptions, such as the UCLA example. More recently, at Paris-Descartes University in France, thousands of bodies donated for research were reported sold for unethical purposes or stored in poor conditions for more than a decade, many piled up on gurneys, decomposing, and being gnawed by mice. Also, research institutions are sometimes the buyers in transactions with body brokers. Once bodies are accepted by brokers, they're dismembered and shipped to national and international clients for research and education, often in postgraduate training programs.

Medical schools in Pennsylvania and Florida believe the scandals around body brokerages have resulted in reduced donations to their legitimate institutional programs.

Champney says that isn't the case for all med schools, but he continues to warn the public against for-profit body brokers: "If (people) do really want to donate their loved one, there are other alternatives which are much more ethical and much more moral."

It is sometimes difficult, however, to know exactly who you're donating to and where your body will end up. The process of donation varies from state to state. In Massachusetts, people donate bodies directly to medical schools like Boston University. In other states with central anatomical boards, a person would donate a body to a clearing house for bodies, which then allocates cadavers or parts. "I would hate for people to see the word 'medical' and think it's all the same thing," says Dr. Ann Zumwalt of the clearing houses.

"The tricky thing is in the US that the federal laws are relatively loose and state laws vary widely in how strict they are." As a result, it is possible to accidentally donate bodies to companies that use donated cadavers for other than legitimate medical reasons.

Anatomists say governments must take action to end the confusion and the travesties. The American medical community accuses state and national governments of being irresponsibly remiss. Author Goodwin says that the federal government and bioethicists have been in denial about the underground market at work, failing both to ask where the body parts are coming from, and to regulate the trade.

Some legislators are taking heed. The Uniform Anatomical Gift Act, first passed in 1968 and updated twice since, is the law that prohibits the sale or purchase of human body parts in the United States. Two congressmen have introduced a bipartisan bill to reinforce the act. Democrat Bobby Rush of Illinois and Florida Republican Gus Bilirakis want to create a registration and tracking system for body and body parts donated for research, preventing brokers and bad actors from taking advantage of donors and their families. "Individuals and families who make the selfless decision to advance scientific research must be certain that the remains of their loved ones will be treated with the utmost dignity and respect," says Rush. Adds Bilirakis, "Measures to ensure accountability and transparency in this process are much-needed on a federal level."

Dr. Callum Ross, an anatomist at the University of Chicago, is sceptical that the bill would make a difference. A registry has been tried before, he says, without much success. The bill's content is about "a bunch of stuff like packaging and labelling," no more effective than "changing the paintwork on the Titanic."

Each state also has rules on procurement and handling of bodies. Some have anatomical boards or health departments to manage donations; others allow direct donation to accredited medical schools, which have staff on site to handle storage, identification, and final disposition of remains.

Part of the problem with existing laws at the state and national level is enforcement. The University of Miami's Champney believes governments need to take a much stronger role in applying the law or, at a minimum, regulating the treatment of human remains and best practices in the ethical use of willed bodies. Chicago's Ross agrees, noting that federal law enforcement prefers to deal with what they regard as more compelling crimes such as sex and drug trafficking. Investigation of crimes involving profiteering in human bodies and body parts is more likely to devolve to individual states, he says. "There are plenty of laws in place within the states to punish bad actors, but states attorneys aren't educated in these laws. They're the ones who should be taking care of this. But how can they prosecute if they don't know what's going on?"

There appears to be a general idea in the United States, says Champney, "that once you're dead, you're property. You have no more rights than an old refrigerator. As soon as an individual dies, if you want to do research on them there are no rules or regulations." There are Federal Trade Commission Rules for funeral homes, "but if you're not a funeral home, you don't fall under those rules."

Champney has called for basic foundational regulations governing all human tissue. "Whether you're talking about someone's liver or someone's body," he says, "they should all fall under rules of human tissue use." The differing state rules

133

amount to "a hodgepodge," he says. "And body brokers don't want change because they're making lots of money." He suggests the United States adopt a model similar to those used in the United Kingdom and New Zealand which have very strong rules about use of human tissue. There's little news of an active body-broker business in Canada, perhaps because of its public health-care system, which tends to discourage such for-profit activities.

In the meantime, unregulated body brokers are a facet of American society that consumers can live–or die–without. It is up to individuals to consider the inadvisability of dealing with for-profit "anatomical science" businesses. Tread carefully before making crucial end-of-life decisions and maybe consider making them earlier rather than later. People who donate their bodies to medical school programs usually make the donation ten years before they die, says Champney, while those who donate to body brokers make the decision more spontaneously.

Again, if money is a concern, many of the same financial benefits are available at legitimate medical schools as from private brokers. What's not available from the for-profit players is a guarantee that bodies will be handled in a respectable, dignified, and responsible manner, or even assurance that they'll be used in relation to serious anatomical medical science.

CHAPTER TWELVE

Hard truths about funeral homes

"Funerals are expensive, broken and exploitative. They have to change."
—Nicole Archer, social media producer, CNET (2020).

Older boomers are now likely to be coping with heart disease, stroke, or other causes of infirmity. Even though their smoking rates have declined, they are being diagnosed with cancer, heart disease, and diabetes, plus forms of dementia, not to mention COVID-19 and its variants. Some will die from a combination of what the health-care professions call comorbidities, a combination of several ailments, while others die simply as a result of the normal aging process. Whatever the diagnosis, the final result is the same and a friend, family member, or caregiver will in most cases wind up calling a funeral home.

Funeral directors and those who work for them don't have the easiest of jobs. They're generally are on call 24/7, performing a valuable, often stressful, and not always appreciated service. Those in the field have knowledge that can help and support families when they need it most. They labour tirelessly to keep up with demand. At least one study has shown that stress and depression are common among funeral directors and those who work for them.

A 2019 Harvard University research study by sociologist Jessica McClanahan focused on the trauma that mortuary workers are directly exposed to through body handling and preparation. "They may also face additional work stressors in their dealings with the bereaved," she wrote. "Through bereavement and counselling, mortuary workers may also be exposed to aversive details of trauma to the deceased or become fatigued by the emotional weight of their counselling duties." There's reason to believe that many of these individuals meet clinical criteria for trauma exposure, McClanahan wrote.

Civilian mortuary workers are perhaps not exposed to traumatic death as frequently or severely as those in military or disaster situations. But their exposure is ongoing throughout their careers. They may see bodies that have come to unnatural ends such as homicide, suicide, automotive accident, drowning, and fire. Interacting with the families of these victims adds to trauma.

McClanahan points to unique social issues mortuary workers may face. Historically, working with the dead was assigned to lower social classes. While this may no longer be the case, the stigma still lingers and "morticians and funeral directors are painfully aware of the common negative stereotype of people in their occupations," she wrote. An earlier survey of funeral directors in four states found mortuary workers particularly stigmatized "not only because they perform work that few others would be willing to do, but also because they profit from death."

While rituals have death have evolved in many ways since pre-Biblical times, in the last century or two, the funeral business, also known as the bereavement sector, has become a mammoth industry. Its growth has not always been for the best of reasons, or with the best of intentions, or with the best results for families. That's not a reflection on all funeral directors or funeral homes. As in any line of business, there are good and bad, and it *is* a business, one that many of us will rely on when the time comes.

Caleb Wilde is the forty-year-old descendent of six generations of funeral directors. The family has been in the business since the mid-1800s. He not only manages the Wilde Funeral Home in Parkesburg, a town of 3,500 in eastern Pennsylvania, he often answers the phone.

Wilde is also known for his award-winning book, *Confessions of a Funeral Director: How Death Saved My Life*, his blog of the same title, and his appearance on YouTube. He's won a devoted following with his often-humorous online posts dealing with the topic of death. He refers to his blog as "irreverent, yes, insensitive, no." (A second book, *All the Ways Our Dead Still Speak*, published in 2022, deals with the funeral director's perspectives on life, death, and the hereafter.) Wilde can also be an outspoken critic of his industry.

"Not only is it unfriendly to the environment, it's also unfriendly to the way we approach death," he said in a TEDx Talk. "The professionalism of death-care has brought us some wonderful things. But there are sustainable options that are environmentally friendly and death-embracing."

Wilde's writing doesn't mask the fact that he struggles constantly with depression, burnout, and stress. Being faced almost daily with death, especially the death of children, has been extremely difficult for him. And he knows he's not alone. Along with the typical challenges, Wilde says, much of the mental burden borne by funeral service workers is caused by bosses and co-workers who don't understand stress management techniques. He tries to create a working environment at the Wilde Funeral Home where employees can share their needs and emotions. At one time, he confesses, he was ashamed of his depression, which had shaken his spiritual beliefs. But he's since learned to not just "work around it, but to work with it." Wilde adds, "The more that we embrace life, the more we can embrace death."

There is a fair amount of work to be done when someone passes, which is usually where funeral directors enter the picture. Once a doctor or qualified nurse practitioner has made the death pronouncement, proper procedures must be followed. The body must be transported to the burial location, crematory, or other location selected. It is generally washed, dressed, and cooled. A timeline should be established to obtain all permits and authorizations, notify family and friends, allow for any cultural or religious observances, and prepare for the preferred disposition method. "There's only one chance to get the funeral right," wrote funeral consumer advocate Josh Slocum in his book *Final Rights.* "Since most of us will never arrange for more than one or two funerals, you won't have much practice."

Families have the right to make final decisions around how a funeral will be handled, especially if the deceased has provided written instructions before their death, and they are not always required to engage a funeral home to provide services or to transfer the body but that varies from jurisdiction to jurisdiction. Some states, for instance, require a funeral director be hired to file the death certificate, receive a body from a hospital, sign transfer permits, and oversee disposition; others require a funeral director only when the deceased had a contagious disease. Also, municipalities and individual cemeteries, crematories, and other disposition facilities may or may not have their own requirements for funeral directors.

Whether or not a funeral director is not used, the death certificate must be registered, usually within a specified number of days. Registering a death requires two principal documents. A medical certificate of death, completed by an attending doctor, coroner, or other authority, outlines the cause of death. If the person dies in a facility like a hospital or nursing home, the staff will usually see that this declaration is made. If the death occurs at home, the relatives need to immediately contact local emergency officials to take the deceased to a facility where a legal declaration of death can be made. Family members who die in hospice care can be declared dead by staff. The time for filing a death certificate varies, but it must be completed before other permits are issued and before final disposition.

The second document is a statement of death. This form is usually completed by the funeral director and an informant (usually a family member). It includes personal information about the deceased, such as family history, age, and place of death.

(The process of registering a death is a reminder that it is helpful to one's survivors to make available or known all of the following: last will, insurance policies, unpaid bills or debts, bank account numbers, online or credit card access codes or numbers, driver's license, vehicle ownership papers, government social or old-age security plans, income tax contacts, deeds to property, pension information, health-care policy numbers and public health card, locations of family histories, subscriptions.)

When a funeral director is retained, he or she will submit the statement of death and medical certificate of death to the municipal clerk's office, usually in the municipality where the death occurred. The information gathered about causes of death may be used for medical/health research or statistics. A death must be registered before a burial permit can be issued. (Most funeral directors handle this, too.) The permit is required for a cremation, burial, or alkaline hydrolysis.

If the family is not using a funeral service provider, a family member must get the completed medical certificate of death from the medical practitioner when taking charge of the remains. The statement of death form, available from the municipal clerk's office, needs to be filled out and filed, along with the medical certificate of death, to the municipal clerk's office.

A burial permit, if applicable, will also need to be acquired. If the family is not using a funeral service provider, the municipality where the death is registered can help get a burial permit. It is issued at the time the death is registered. There are various state, provincial, or local laws that stipulate the time period in which all this must be completed.

Certified copies of the filed death certificate are needed to conduct a number of other tasks. Without one, a permit to transport the body to the place of disposition can't be issued, to say nothing of the insurance, pension, and estate issues that can't proceed.

The body can be brought directly to a family home from a hospital or residential care facility, but the transfer must be authorized by the executor or next of kin. If a death occurs in the home, there's no need to move the body immediately. Keep in mind, though, there is a need to protect those handling the body from unknowingly being exposed to health risks. If the person died from a contagious disease, the family must consult a doctor.

Much of the difficulty involved in funerals can be mitigated through advance care planning. Think of it as the end-of-life equivalent of car insurance. No one plans to have a car accident, but insurance is essential in the event. Serious illness or an accident can easily leave anyone incapacitated and unable to make decisions. Having an advance care plan, or advance health-care directive, as they are sometimes known, is invaluable when you are unable to express your wishes or preferences. Although it may never be needed, such a document ensures one's wishes are followed by health-care providers and family. Discussing wishes in advance with family members or close friends, as well as health-care providers, should be part of the process.

An advance directive, living will, or power of attorney articulates and documents one's wishes regarding medical treatment. An example is to state preferences about when to withhold or withdraw life-sustaining treatment, whether or not one wants artificially provided nutrition or hydration when close to death or unconscious, and do-not-resuscitate orders. The directive may also include information about what procedures one requires upon their death and general statements about end-of-life care, preferences for body disposition, organ or full-body donation, and any plans for memorials or services. A trusted person can be chosen as a substitute decision maker or health-care agent or proxy to make medical and disposition choices. The ideal person should know the individual well, be able to make decisions under pressure, and be nearby when the need arises.

An advance directive must include the contact person of the health-care agent or proxy, and answers to specific questions about one's preferences for care. It can also contain the names and signatures of individuals who witness its signing. Not all jurisdictions require these signatures. Taking the time to prepare an advance directive lessens the burden on the family and/or funeral director at a critical time.

While the rituals of death have evolved in many ways since pre-biblical times, in the last 100 to 150 years, the funeral business, known as the bereavement sector, has become a mammoth industry. That's not always been for the best of reasons, nor always with the best of intentions. And it hasn't always produced the best results.

There are now three basic categories of funeral homes: the big, often multinational corporations that increasingly dominate the business; smaller, often family-owned operations; and co-operative associations which are owned by their members. There are legitimate, fair-minded, and respectful practitioners in all three types of organization, and there are expensive, aggressive, and even predatory operators in both the large and small funeral homes (more on this in the next chapter).

The big players, some of which have revenues in the billions, include Service International Corporation, Matthews International, Carriage Services, Hillenbrand Industries, Stonemor Operating LLC, Security National, and Canada's Park Lawn Corporation. Most provide full services, including cremation, cemetery accommodation, and merchandise and/or financial services.

Most of the corporations have grown by rolling up smaller operators into chains of funeral homes which benefit from economies of scale and can be quite profitable for their shareholders. Funeral Ethics Organization director Lisa Carlson says the big players tend to view the death industry as a cash cow and often operate with monthly quotas and revenue targets. They are usually more expensive than family-owned companies or co-operatives, and they have a reputation for dubious business practices that often leave people looking for alternatives.

Independent family or co-op owned-and-operated funeral homes take pride in their services and tend to spend more time with their staff on integrity and trust, and less time "upselling" services and products. Like any business, turning a profit is part of the equation. But their staff aren't normally required to meet sales quotas to ensure quarterly bonuses.

In the United Kingdom, the National Society of Allied and Independent Funeral Directors is an 870-member organization of independent funeral homes, privately owned businesses run by small teams. The association says most of its members are family-run outfits, many in business for generations, and they pride themselves on their quality of customer service. "Unfortunately," the UK society notes, "it's not always easy to tell the difference between an independent funeral director and a large national chain, especially if you're not familiar with the funeral industry. Yet, who owns the funeral home can entirely change the experience of arranging a funeral, from what you can expect to pay right up to the quality of the funeral itself."

Caleb Wilde believes the funeral business lends itself to local ownership and control. The chief concern of operators should be on helping families through their grief rather than making money. "We know our people," he says. "We grew up here."

Stephen Garrett, a former corporate funeral industry employee, now an end-of-life coach and author, has seen both sides and has a definite preference for "all those amazing family-run funeral homes that are offering affordable, graceful, dignified end-of-life services."

Independent operators are predominant in smaller markets. The corporate chains aren't interested in small towns. An area with 200 or less deaths in a year doesn't generate enough revenue to produce the expected return on investment for shareholders.

Funeral co-operatives are membership-based organizations that function within communities to meet the needs of mourning families. Their aim is to serve families regardless of their spending ability, promote education, and encourage members to make funeral arrangements in advance without emotional strain. They are democratic organizations, controlled by members who establish their policies and make all decisions. Memberships are usually open to all. Profits are normally shared with members.

Funeral co-operatives are just beginning to get traction in the United States. One of the few co-ops now operating was founded in 1929 in the small city of New Ulm, Minnesota. Established by residents of the Minnesota Valley to provide affordable burials during the Great Depression, it has a membership of 5,000. It still charges a mere $5 for membership. As of 2021, it hadn't raised its prices in more than four years. Its profits, after costs, are shared with members who use the service in any given year. Like other co-ops, its members vote on how it operates. Farming communities like New Ulm are already familiar with co-ops, a corporate structure often used to manage crops, produce, and grocery outlets.

Another American co-op is the People's Memorial Association, a non-profit which has served the greater Seattle and Kings County communities since 1939. With a membership of over 70,000, making it the largest single co-op in North America, the association contracts with funeral homes across the state to provide members with discounted funeral and cremation services. A lifetime membership costs $50 with no annual premiums.

Outraged by the steep prices and high-pressure sales tactics of the corporate funeral home industry, the members of People's Memorial Association decided in 2007 to also open their own funeral home in response to the US giant Service Corporation International (SCI) purchasing locally owned funeral homes in the region. SCI increased its prices and cancelled contracts the association had with these businesses before they were bought. The association ensures that all companies it partners with abide by its code of conduct, says its executive director, Amanda Stock. "Its focus is on education so that people can have access to information and options available to them so they can make choices that are best for them and their family," she said. "We also want to make sure that many options are available." That's why it supported the legalization of alternatives to burial and cremation like alkaline hydrolysis and natural organic reduction (or composting) in Washington State. "They're just other disposition options that might be meaningful to people," Stock says.

The group conducts a funeral home price survey every two years in Washington State. Most recently, it found the cost of cremation ranges from $600 to over $4,000. And some funeral homes were charging from $5,000 to over $15,000 for a burial, not including the cost of a cemetery plot and casket.

Unlike corporate funeral homes, People's Memorial doesn't prioritize pre-payment. The funeral industry has done "a good job promoting prepayment as something everyone should do," Stock suggested, "but the reality is that pre-payment mostly benefits the funeral industry." It's a good practice for people who don't have survivors they trust to handle the funeral bill when they die. Otherwise, Stock encourages people "to pre-plan and talk with their family and loved ones about their wishes. If they want to set money aside, it's better for the individual to just use a savings account if they have someone they trust to be listed as the beneficiary to withdraw the funds to pay the funeral home when the time comes." The next best thing, she says, is to set up a life insurance policy to pay funeral expenses.

There are reports of growing interest in co-ops in the United States, partly due to COVID-19 which took so many lives in a short period of time and strained the capacities of the existing system. The director in New Ulm, Eric Warmka, told Minnesota Public Radio his organization has been getting more calls of late for information on how to found and run a co-op. People's Memorial has fielded similar requests. "It is not the easiest way to set up a business and you need community engagement to make it work," Stock concedes. "I hope it's a growing movement, but I don't see evidence yet of others opening up in the US." Money is a constraint. It's important for their initial success that co-ops have solid up-front capital or they're not likely to flourish, one co-op official warns.

In addition to frustration with the rising costs of funerals and disillusionment with the corporate funeral industry, one factor that might spark greater interest among Americans in co-ops is the sheer number of boomers considering their last wishes. "The boomer generation," says Stock, "is an information generation and they're going to be more educated about their options than their parents were."

Although not widely accepted yet in the United States, funeral co-operatives are a growing movement in Canada. Six provinces have funeral co-ops, including Quebec, New Brunswick, Prince Edward Island, Manitoba, Alberta, and three in Ontario.

The Co-operative Memorial Society in Alberta has served 46,000 members in the Calgary area since its creation in 1965. It has 15,000 members. Its funerals average $2,500 (CAD). The Federation of Funeral Cooperatives of Quebec is an umbrella organization for over thirty individual co-ops with a combined total of 170,000 members. Some of these co-ops operate out of province, and others still have associates as far away as Peru, Puerto Rico, and France. At least one Quebec co-op offers alkaline hydrolysis and some operate their own cemeteries.

The Canadian co-ops "didn't like the idea of big US funeral corporations profiting from the deaths of Quebecers or Canadians," says Louis Grenier, secretary of the Calgary-based co-op. While two co-ops in Quebec bought out funeral homes from Service Corporation International, most of them don't actually own funeral homes, but purchase services from other independents. "It's a good solution to a long-term problem," Grenier says.

In Manitoba, locals set up their own funeral co-op in 1997 after a big big-name funeral home jacked prices up by 15 percent. "If that's happening in other communities where people are just tired of what's going on," death-care consultant and funeral director Shane Neufeld says, "then it wouldn't surprise me if we'll see a bunch of co-ops."

Political support for co-operative funeral services has grown significantly, particularly in the United Kingdom, where Labour Party members got behind it.

Home funerals

The home funeral is an increasingly popular alternative to the conventional funeral or corporate funeral option. Often intimate, loving, and affordable, home funerals can be carried out legally and safely in most jurisdictions.

Families have the right to provide their own after-death care but are required to make arrangements with a local municipality, usually where the death occurred. Proper procedures must be followed, including completing necessary paperwork and adhering to state, provincial, or local laws. There are time frames in which all this is to be accomplished. The death must be officially pronounced as soon as possible by a doctor or by qualified nursing practitioner, who completes forms certifying the cause, the time, and the place of death, enabling an official death certificate to be issued.

It is important to know the medical history of the deceased when planning a home funeral to protect those handling the body from unwittingly being exposed to health risks. If the person died from a contagious disease, the family must consult a doctor. The deceased may have informed the family of a wish that the body or its organs be donated. In addition to the permits and authorizations, family and friends must be notified, accommodations made for cultural or religious observances, and preparations for the preferred method of disposition.

If family members wish to perform these duties, preparation of the body includes washing and dressing it, as well as providing a casket or shroud. The body must be kept cool, requiring ice packs or dry ice or other cooling products placed around vital organs. People must be prepared for rigor mortis. The body can be brought directly to a family home from a hospital or residential care facility, but the transfer must be authorized by the executor or next-of-kin. If a death occurs in the home, there's no need to move the body immediately.

Advocates of home funerals realize that caring for a deceased family member is not always an easy task, but resources are available. The US-based National Home Funeral Association Association's was founded to educate and support individuals, families, and communities in caring for their dead. Created in 2010, its members come from all fifty states, five Canadian provinces, and seven countries.

A family may retain the services of clergy or a death doula (home funeral guide) who is trained to know the law, help find resources, and provide other services. Usually women, the doulas advocate for funerals led by and centred on family. They do not actually conduct after-death care. Their role is to ensure the most meaningful care is carried out by family and/or friends. The services of death doulas are regarded by many as invaluable. They charge fees in keeping with fair business practices of equitable compensation for services.

Regardless of whether a funeral is conducted through a funeral director, through a co-operative, or at home, many of the same environmental concerns are relevant. Two of the least eco-friendly activities associated with funerals are driving long distances to attend and the purchase of flowers, particularly imported ones.

It goes without saying that travelling (by car, plane, or train) to attend memorials can come with an environmental cost depending on distance. Families may appreciate other sensible ways of receiving condolences. Many funeral homes are installing technology for remote viewing or live streaming of services, particularly since COVID-19.

Sending flowers to grieving families is a traditional gesture. But flowers for funeral and memorial services have been called a beautiful waste. They don't last. And importing flowers from countries like Columbia makes little environmental sense. Worse, as the web portal SevenPonds.com points out, some of the large-scale flower farms in South and Central America use pesticides banned in North America. Floriculture in some countries can expose water sources, bird and animal populations, and low-paid workers, many of them children, to toxic chemicals, with predictably negative effects.

Some flowers and arrangements can be chosen with fewer unfortunate consequences. The florist can be asked to provide certification that flowers or potted plants were produced responsibly. Pesticide-free, organic flowers can be purchased from local growers or ordered online (the closer the provider, the better).

An often-used alternative to flowers is the financial donation, usually to the deceased's preferred charity. The eco-minded might also ask for plants or trees. They not only last but help the planet rather than hurt it.

Just as there is almost no way to entirely eliminate the environmental cost of a funeral, there is no escaping some financial cost. As the cost of living rises so, too, does the cost of dying. Society will need to find better ways to manage this as larger segments of the population die off in the coming years. As mentioned earlier, "funeral poverty" is affecting families no matter where they live. Few have set aside money for unexpected costs such as a death in the family. But people struggling with low incomes or heavy debt do have options, some more palatable than others.

Naturally, the best way to save on funeral or disposition expenses is to plan ahead. For those who haven't, often families and friends are the best resort. In the Internet age, crowdfunding has grown as an option, although families may, out of pride, have reservations about using it. Some funeral providers offer payment plans. There are also companies that specialize in loans for burials or other options, but the interest rates can be steep. Most funeral homes want to be paid up front, and many won't perform services without payment.

Lower-cost options for disposition such as direct access to a crematory were reviewed in earlier chapters.

Some local or state governments offer indigent disposition for low-income families. A family can consult a county coroner's office, which may provide funds for cremation or burial upon signing a release. In worst cases, the deceased are buried in mass graves, such as Hart Island in New York. Indigents buried this way are often simply identified as "John or Jane Doe." Although they're not personalized, even with indigent burials, ceremonies are often offered to honour the dead.

In the United States, only the surviving spouse or child qualifies for the federal death benefit of $255. It applies if the survivor was living with the deceased or receiving spousal benefits. A lump sum payment can go to an eligible son or daughter at home, offspring still in school, or disabled. The one-time death benefit should not be confused with survivor benefits paid to family members on an ongoing basis.

The Canada Pension Plan (CPP) provides a payment of up to $2,500 (CAD) to the estate of the deceased, provided they qualify. The amount depends on how long the deceased contributed to the CPP. But no Canadian family is denied the dignity of a funeral. If they're not eligible for the CPP death benefit, provincial or municipal governments will help cover basic expenses. A funeral home will usually help with these applications, whether or not its services are used.

In the United Kingdom, some believe death-care should be provided under the National Health Service, an idea that might be considered by other countries, provided the political appetite exists.

In New Zealand, when a family member dies, the next of kin may get assistance with the cost of the funeral, burial, or cremation. In some cases, help may be available with living expenses or childcare. The Funeral Directors Association (FDA) of New Zealand is urging the government to increase the benefits for low-income funerals. The current New Zealand Funeral Grant of $1,461 covers only about 37 percent of the cost of a simple funeral. The FDA wants the grant increased to $4,037.

In Australia, the type and amount of bereavement payment depends on individual circumstances, relationship to the deceased, and when notification of the death is received. In most cases, submitting a claim is not required. The executor of the estate can access the benefit from a bank account.

Much could change about funerals by the time we hit 2040 and the decade of departure. If current trends hold, we could see more people taking control of the end-of-life processes, bringing relatives home to die, interring them in natural burial grounds, and mourning them online and in other ways. Boomers will have their own ideas about how to manage things, and their children are also likely to weigh in on methods of disposal and the conduct of funereal rites. Social attitudes and religious values and environmental concerns will likely continue to evolve. Regardless, funeral directors and funeral homes are likely to continue to be an important part of the death-services world for decades to come. Here, as in so many other things, researching options and choosing a provider in advance may save a great deal of trouble later. As American funeral consumer-rights advocate Josh Slocum wrote in *Final Rights*: "there's only one chance to get the funeral right. Since most of us will never arrange for more than one or two funerals, you won't have much practice."

CHAPTER THIRTEEN

The corporate way of death

"You may not be able to change the world, but at least you can embarrass the guilty."

—Jessica Mitford

For centuries, the death-care industry has been haunted by revelations of sharp practices and extreme profit-seeking. Indeed, the Victorian trope of the greedy funeral director–often a wealthy miser lacking scruples and motivated only by money–is still with us today, in large part because, then as now, it's not entirely fiction. Ripping people off at sad and vulnerable moments in their lives is beyond reproach, but not beyond reality.

Jessica Mitford updated a lot of the historic criticisms of the bereavement industry in her 1963 bestseller (revised in a 1998 edition) *The American Way of Death*. It documented the many ways in which funeral directors took advantage of grieving friends and family to convince them to overpay for services. She foresaw the rise of the profit-oriented funeral chains that have since devoured thousands of mom-and-pop operations.

Mitford's investigations brought changes to American law designed to protect consumers from unscrupulous practitioners. She can't be said to have stopped the abuse in its tracks, however. It might be a stretch to imagine the big guns of the dismal trade rubbing their hands in anticipation of the end of a baby-boom generation but their focus continues to be more on price points and corporate returns than on grieving families. Books that are more recent and revealing than Mitford's, including several insider accounts by independent practitioners of the trade, some now retired, show how little has changed.

"Just to be clear," wrote Caleb Wilde in *Confessions of a Funeral Director*, "I, like most independent funeral directors don't like corporate-run funeral homes. I think they're bad for consumers, and they hurt the already injured perception of the funeral industry by perpetuating the money-hungry mortician stereotype."

Wilde's opinion was shared by long-retired funeral director Darryl Roberts, who wrote in his book *Profits of Death* (1997) that for years giant corporations have been gobbling up the mom-and-pop funeral homes at a "voracious" rate. "The buying-power advantage of a conglomerate is obvious," Roberts wrote. "But if a conglomerate has control of an entire segment of the market, will those savings be passed on to the consumer? That doesn't appear to be the case."

Two years before Roberts' book was published, Service International Corporation (SCI), the biggest funeral company in the world, had annual revenues of over $1.5 billion and employed 15,000. By 2021, SCI's total revenue had reached $4.14 billion, up 17.9 percent from the previous year. Big funeral corporations are still the minority of the roughly 20,000 funeral homes in the United States, 1,700 in Canada, and 7,000 in the United Kingdom, but they are by far the fastest-growing segment of the market.

Since its founding in 1962, SCI has bought out hundreds of family-owned funeral homes. The bulk of its revenue is generated by operations in the United States and Canada. (Its UK arm operates as Dignity Plc.) Headquartered near Houston, Texas, it operates under several names with more than 1,500 funeral homes and 400 cemeteries in forty-three US states, eight Canadian provinces, and Puerto Rico.

Though some media describe SCI as "the Wal-Mart" of the funeral industry, the comparison doesn't quite hold. "Unlike Wal-Mart, SCI's economies of scale don't translate into cost savings for consumers," the Funeral Consumers Alliance says. A survey conducted by the FCA and the Consumer Federation of America revealed that SCI's median prices are "significantly higher" than independently owned funeral homes.

SCI was involved in a 1990s controversy involving alleged violations of embalming laws in Texas. This became a political issue due to a company executive's friendship with (and contributions to) the family of then-governor and later president George W. Bush. The media, inevitably, dubbed it "Funeralgate" (or "Formaldegate"). A lawsuit against SCI over the alleged violations was settled for $200,000.

Around the same time, it came to light that workers at SCI's Memorial Gardens cemetery near Fort Lauderdale buried people in the wrong places, broke open vaults to squeeze in other remains, and, in some instances, tossed bones into the woods. The cemetery employees had oversold plots and run out of space. Bodies were stacked on top of each other and remains relocated without notifying relatives. The allegations particularly appalled observant Jewish customers. (Under Jewish law, bodies must be buried intact and undisturbed.)

SCI agreed to settle the Fort Lauderdale suit for $100 million, which was distributed among 350 families and their lawyers. In addition to that payout, SCI reached a $14 million agreement with the state attorney general's office that required the company to repair the plots and reorganize the cemeteries to ensure graves were properly marked and could be accommodated.

The *Washington Post* ran a series of stories about SCI in the aughts. One was about the burial of a stillborn child in an eight-inch-deep grave. Another reported that an SCI facility was storing decomposing naked bodies in "disgusting, degrading, and humiliating" conditions." Among the hundreds of bodies stored on makeshift gurneys and shelves in an unrefrigerated garage were deceased veterans awaiting burial at Arlington National Cemetery.

A 2009 class-action suit against SCI and a Jewish cemetery it managed, Eden Memorial Park in Mission Hills, California, alleged that managers at the cemetery broke as many as 1,500 buried concrete vaults in order to fit more bodies in, and discarded or lost human skulls and other remains in a "dump area." SCI denied wrongdoing but agreed to a settlement of $80.5 million.

Yahoo News recently reported that SCI's cremation services agreed to pay up to $209 million in refunds to settle a federal class-action lawsuit alleging it deceived 87,000 Florida customers who purchased its prepaid plans. SCI Direct Inc., formerly called Neptune Society Management Corp., was named as co-defendant in the class-action. An attorney for the plaintiff said consumers spent an average $2,400 each for end-of-life services, including an insurance policy guaranteeing that if the purchaser dies while travelling, the body will be returned to Florida from anywhere in the world.

The lawsuit accused the companies of violating Florida laws that require prepaid cremation services providers to deposit 70 percent of prepaid funds into a trust and provide 100 percent refunds for the services upon request. It also accused the companies of unjust enrichment and violations of the state's Deceptive and Unfair Trade Practices Act. Florida established the requirement to hold 70 percent of purchase prices in a trust because of the possibility that cremation-services providers might not still be in business when needed years or decades after the purchases. It also required full refunds in case purchasers move out of state or change their minds about wanting to be cremated.

The lawsuit accused the companies of reducing the amount of money they were required to put into a trust by requiring customers to sign two contracts, one for the cremation services and another for related merchandise. It claimed that while the wholesale value of the merchandise sent to customers was $25 or less, the company logged its collective value as "incredibly high," including $498 for a memory chest, $329 for an urn, $199 for a keepsake plaque, and $185 for a planning guide. At the same time, the companies reduced the value of the cremation services in its logs to an amount far below what they would have had to report if consumers bought just the cremation services, the suit stated.

Under the settlement, which still must be approved by a judge, refunds will be made available to all Florida consumers who purchased its pre-need funeral agreements, transportation, and relocation protection plans and related retail merchandise agreements since April 2016. How many of the 87,000 customers will request refunds remains uncertain. SCI and its affiliates denied the lawsuit's allegations. "While we strongly maintain there was no wrongdoing on Neptune's behalf," said a spokesman, "in an effort to move forward and continue our full focus on serving our families, we agreed to settle the remaining disputes."

While there have been still other controversies involving SCI, it must be noted that the company is hardly the only large funeral firm to be accused of dubious practices. In April 2022, the US Department of Justice, acting on behalf of the Federal Trade Commission, announced that it was suing Funeral & Cremation Group of North America, Legacy Cremation Services, and Heritage Cremation Provider, among others, for "misrepresenting their location and prices, illegally threatening and failing to return cremated remains to consumers, and failing to provide disclosures required by the [US] Funeral Rule."

The defendants, according to the DOJ suit, frequently posed as local providers when they weren't, and charged consumers more than their posted prices. When consumers resisted undisclosed fees and price increases, the companies in question allegedly held the remains hostage. Said Samuel Levine, director of the FTC's Bureau of Consumer Protection,

"Preying on consumers when they are dealing with the loss of a loved one is outrageous, and it's illegal."

The Funeral Rule mentioned in the DOJ suit was enacted by the US Federal Trade Commission (FTC) in 1984 and updated a decade later. It was inspired, in part, by Mitford's book. "The rule," as it's known, is intended to protect consumers from unethical and often outrageous practices by giving consumers adequate information about services and products, including pricing and so-called "pre-need" arrangements.

Under the Funeral Rule, funeral directors are required to provide their price lists to families at the beginning of funeral discussions. Consumers have the right to purchase services and products item-by-item, selecting only what they need. They have the right to decline embalming. They are free to call around to other funeral homes seeking better prices or services.

The Funeral Rule also stipulates that a funeral home cannot insist a customer buy a funeral package or pay for everything included in a package. It must make a full price list available on request, including the costs of lower priced urns and caskets. A funeral home cannot refuse a casket or urn purchased elsewhere, nor charge a fee for the use of a casket or urn purchased elsewhere. A casket is not required for cremation and a funeral home cannot require one.

The intent of the Funeral Rule is to "address the imbalance between the buyer, who is grieving, and the vendor, who is in a rational and businesslike frame of mind," says the Funeral Consumers Alliance. The FCA advises individuals and families to take a realistic look at their budgets before calling a funeral home and decide what they can reasonably afford without sacrificing funds for daily living.

The alliance has repeatedly urged the Federal Trade Commission to give the rule more teeth. "The funeral industry's reluctance to operate transparently and competitively will not be remedied without more effective and up-to-date government regulations." it says "Revisions to the rule that we propose are fair, they comport with common sense and they pose little or no financial burden to the industry." It would have the funeral industry post price lists on a funeral home's website, something neither burdensome nor costly, yet helpful to consumers seeking to comparison shop (only 18 percent of more than a thousand US funeral homes surveyed in 2022 post price lists.) "Online price posting would benefit not just those consumers searching for price information, but also encouraging price competition and discouraging funeral homes from charging exorbitant prices," says Stephen Brobeck of the Consumer Federation of America.

The FTC announced in 2020 that it is considering an update to the rule to improve price competition, although it has yet to commit to mandated online price-posting. Surveys and research reveal differences in prices of up to 400 and 500 percent for the same funeral services.

However toothless the rule may be, it's better than nothing. Regrettably, few other countries have adopted similar regulations. Dubious practices by corporate funeral giants are by no means unique to the United States. They are rife in countries where governments tend to take a largely hands-off approach to the industry.

Australia's $1 billion (AUD) funeral sector is not immune to shady players. Whitsunday Funeral and Crematorium is a family-owned business that operates funeral homes in Queensland. It is regarded as one of the most reputable in the area. But owner Jeff Boyle had little good to say about some of his competitors. In a television interview, Boyle claimed that many facilities use fake tops to cover cheap coffins used for cremations. Some, he said, switch coffins at the last minute, often with pine or fibreboard boxes, without informing customers.

The *Daily Mail Australia* reported bodies being embalmed in a garage and human remains dumped down a household drain. An elderly woman's expensive coffin was swapped for a cheap pine box. In another case, a $1,700 (AUD) casket lined with white silk was reportedly switched for a $70 pine box moments before a cremation. "Absolutely disgraceful," said the consumer advocacy group CHOICE, which investigated consumer rip-offs in Australia's funeral industry. Its report also detailed wide discrepancies in pricing among providers.

CHOICE singled out one funeral chain as a particular offender. Invocare posted profits of $40 million (AUD) in 2019. The chain, which operates the White Lady Funerals and Simplicity Funerals brands, has been accused of charging fees for no service, adding unnecessary late fees to bills, and otherwise gouging consumers. "It's just one of the disturbing trends we uncovered in our investigation into an industry plagued with profiteering, hidden fees, and upselling," said CHOICE's Erin Turner. Demands for national standards in the funeral industry are increasingly heard in Australia.

In 2017, the Canadian Broadcasting Corporation's (CBC) *Marketplace* program and the *Toronto Star* newspaper undertook a joint investigation of Arbor Memorial, the largest funeral home chain in Canada. It found markups on caskets and urns averaged 185 percent, depending on the model, and, in some cases, nearly 500 percent. These calculations were based on retail prices at twenty-three Arbor Memorial homes in southern Ontario and a wholesale price list from one large manufacturer.

Posing as relatives, reporters were shown packages for pre-arranged funerals "featuring essential services, such as funeral co-ordination and transferring the body, as well as discretionary services, such as catering, stationery, cars for transporting flowers and chapel staffing." In three instances, Arbor salespeople stated directly to the undercover reporters that all the items, or the vast majority, were necessary. Among the fees was a $340 (CAD) charge to transport a body from a funeral home to a crematorium–on the same property.

Arbor said in a statement at the time that its packaged funeral services provide "good value," are easy to understand, and offer savings. It said an "à la carte" approach is an option. The reporters found that even prices quoted by SCI were lower than those from Arbor.

The regulatory agency in the province of Ontario, the aforementioned Bereavement Authority of Ontario (BAO), has itself come under scrutiny. After an extensive review, Ontario's auditor general, Bonnie Lysyk, released a report in December 2020 that found BAO to be deficient in several of its responsibilities. "Secret shoppers," actually agents from Lysyk's department, visited 100 funeral homes and were met with "sales pressure and/or information giving misleading information." They found that staff (working on commission) attempted to "upsell" clients to buy more expensive products or services. The range in prices offered for basic cremations was staggering–from just over $500 to $8,000 (CAD). The province also found the BAO had taken only "limited action" on 277 cemeteries operating without licenses and failed to monitor more than $2 million (CAD) in care and maintenance for more than 160 others. At the same time that the BAO was being cited by the province for not doing its job, it was being criticized by the funeral sector for bullying and harassing small funeral homes while the corporate chains were said to be operating with relative impunity.

Arbor Memorial also has a leading market share in British Columbia, although SCI controls 54 percent of all funeral homes in the populous lower mainland, says death-care coach Stephen Garrett, who was previously employed by The Memorial Society of British Columbia. Garrett learned a lot about how the big firms operate while earlier employed by SCI: "If you want to see the devil's eyes, get close to him. I lasted a year-and-a half and I quit. I actually got fired because I was too nice."

He recalls a man whose son died of cancer and was being cremated. Garrett gave the dad "a big hug." When he came to pick up his son's cremated remains, Garrett gave him another hug. He says empathy wasn't unusual among his fellow corporate funeral directors. "There's lot of people like that. What I've learned is not to confuse the funeral directors with the culture of [the] corporation they're with." There are some great funeral directors who work for SCI, he says, but most of them are paid by commission, which affects their approach.

Other industry observers back Garrett's observations that not every experience with a corporate-owned funeral home is a bad one, and that there are many corporate funeral directors who prove to be competent, straightforward, and genuinely warm. Even critics such as Caleb Wilde admit that the "corporate monsters" make contributions to the profession. For example, they offer first-generation funeral directors an opportunity to find their first job, and often pay better and offer more days off and more vacation time, provided the employee meets company sales quotas.

Nevertheless, consumers should research who they're dealing with. There's normally a clear difference between genuine, independent, family-owned or co-op funeral homes and the big chains. The giants of the industry often masquerade under the names of small "economy" funeral homes, so it's important to find out if the firm has an investment in the local community or whether it's answerable to an often distant board of directors.

Of course, there are bad actors of the smaller variety, as well. Shane Neufeld, the death-care consultant who has worked for both big and small players, says the chains don't have a monopoly on bad behaviour. "All the things that I saw going on that were the worst tactics were always in privately-owned establishments," he says. "Just because they're independent doesn't mean they're scrupulous." In fact, Neufeld argues that there are some inhibitions on bad behaviour at the big firms that don't pertain to smaller operations. Employees at the chains are expected to adhere to policy manuals that are designed to insulate them from lawsuits. "If anything's going on that's a liability to the organization," Neufeld says, "they want to nip that in the bud. They fear litigation and they have a lot to lose."

While mistreatment of remains and blatant scams get the majority of headlines when it comes to problems in the death-care market, run-of-the-mill greed is the abuse consumers are most likely to encounter, especially in the corporate side of things. "I used to be a corporate finance guy and I know how the corporate mind works," Garrett continues. "They see a million baby boomers in BC and that's times $10,000. That's a $10-billion-dollar payday. So that's what's going on."

The quest for higher returns and big paydays keeps prices generally higher at the corporate funeral chains, and they've been known to increase by as much as 10 percent a year. Grieving families are subjected to aggressive sales pitches for high-end services, caskets, and other arrangements. Some of the services presented as necessary are anything but, starting with embalming.

Many funeral directors, unapologetically and without embarrassment, promote embalming. With few exceptions, it is strictly for profit. In virtually all circumstances, embalming is not only a grotesque and pointless procedure, it is unnecessary in law and for medical reasons. "That's a $600 (CAD) fee," says Stephen Garrett, "and it's not necessary."

The practice began with ancient Egyptians and didn't reach the Americas until the US Civil War, when President Lincoln's body made its final trek from the US Capitol to Illinois and had to be preserved for public viewing. (The trip took nearly three weeks.) The bodies of US Civil War veterans were often also embalmed for transport home.

By the 1950s, embalming was quite common and often performed in the home to make the deceased more suitable for viewing. Embalming is used less frequently today because refrigeration is at least as effective and doesn't require chemicals or invasive procedures. The US Funeral Rule states that embalming is not required by law, except in special cases. In British Columbia, the government has declared that embalming serves no useful purpose in preventing spread of communicable disease.

Former West Virginia funeral director Darryl Roberts describes what takes place during embalming in his book *Profits of Death*:

"The process embalmer must first don a surgical suit and apron, latex gloves, and protective goggles. The body is laid on a table similar to those used for autopsies. Clothing and personal possessions are removed. The body is washed with germicide. Fluid is then removed from the stomach and lungs; the body is often turned over to aide in the procedure. The process of removing gas, fluids, and semi-solids from the body cavities and hollow organs is known as aspiration. The embalmer inserts a long, sharp, hollow instrument, called a trocar, designed for the purpose, into the abdominal cavity to pierce internal organs. The trocar can also be inserted through the nose to remove gas and fluids from the skull.

"Then the arterial embalming process begins. Embalming fluid–a mixture of 40 per cent formaldehyde, water, and other fluids–is pumped into the corpse, while blood from the body is drained onto the table or into sewers. Hypodermic embalming, in which the skin is injected with formaldehyde, and surface embalming, which involves application of embalming fluid to the skin, is also performed.

The purported reasons for embalming are disinfection, preservation, and restoration. Funeral homes often maintain that they must embalm a body to guarantee identification prior to cremation. That's not the case, says Neufeld, if bodies are properly stored in refrigerated conditions (as well, most will come from a medical facility and have an ID wrist band for the purposes of identification).

With rare exceptions, embalming is pushed for profit. It's considered desecration by Muslims, Orthodox Jews, and members of the Bahá'í faith. It has no basis in Christianity. Despite the fact that reputable experts on the disposition of human bodies agree embalming isn't necessary, as do conscientious funeral directors, too many operators of funeral homes insist erroneously and deliberately that embalming is either required by law, necessary to protect the health of the public, or a religious requirement. It isn't.

Funeral homes cannot embalm a body without written

consent. Some require embalming if there is to be a public viewing, but they cannot require embalming for private family services.

Equally contentious, from the points of view of both money and utility, are the containers, usually made of concrete or steel, that enclose a coffin to help prevent a grave from sinking or, worse, caving in. In most of North America, cemeteries and funeral homes highly recommend the use of a burial vault or grave liner, although it's not legally required.

Their use is declining as cremation numbers rise. Which is probably just as well, because the vaults do not decompose (that's the point). Carlton Basmajian of Iowa State University says the materials used to build them, especially concrete, are notoriously environmentally unfriendly. Alterations to the landscape, he says, are made both above ground where insecticides and herbicides are often applied, and below ground, where there's concrete, metal, and toxic chemicals (in the embalmed body). In the United States alone, burial vaults and grave liners consumed more than 14,000 tons of steel and more than 1,636,000 tons of reinforced concrete in 2009.

There are other ways to counter settling earth over a grave. When the casket decomposes or collapses, the cemetery can remedy sunken graves by filling in the settled area. And of course, natural or green burials don't use a casket at all, which means minimal settling.

Many funeral directors will try to sell customers the priciest vault they have. Steel vaults carry the highest profit margins and there are plenty of styles. But Darryl Robert's asked in *Profits of Death*, "what is a vault's purpose?" As the customer, you are told the vault offers additional protection, which begs the question, protection from what? Laughed Roberts: "more protection from those insidious forces of nature: water, bugs, and those pesky gophers."

Another form of aggressive financial pressure placed on families by unscrupulous funeral home operators is the pitch to pay before "time of need." The National Funeral Directors Association continues to advocate pre-paying for a funeral as the best deal for the consumer. People who've prepaid believe they've avoided later problems for their family. But one can plan a funeral in advance without pre-paying. And even the funeral directors' group acknowledges that the industry has received much negative coverage over the pay-ahead practice.

Brett Watson, president of the Funeral Service Association of Canada, calls this an "unfortunate" reflection on the funeral industry. The challenge for funeral directors, he suggests, is recruiting capable, qualified, and responsible staff. "There's going to be negatives that come from certain individuals, but not everybody is like that," says Watson, who manages a Calgary home that's part of the SCI-Dignity chain. "The vast majority of people get into the business because they want to help others. There's a rare instance that something bad happens. It's pretty hard to get into that stuff because of the regulations."

To avoid the problem of missing funds, New York State now requires all prepaid funds be held in trust (in other states, contributors may get back 50 percent percent if they cancel before they need it). In Canada, most funds for pre-arranged funerals are held by a third-party insurance company or in trust in a financial institution.

Paying ahead of time can help families avoid stress and cost when they need it least but the Funeral Consumers Alliance advises that it's better to plan ahead and set money aside rather than pay ahead. A lot can change between the time services are pre-purchased and when they're actually needed, both in your own life and at the funeral home.

"I cannot and will not recommend that most consumers pre-pay," Josh Slocum of the Funeral Consumers Alliance told CBS's *60 Minutes*, adding that the American Association for Retired Persons (AARP) and Consumer Reports agree. "This is standard advice from people who don't have an interest in selling to you, because hundreds of millions of dollars has gone missing, raided from funds over the past few years. If you do feel you have to pre-pay, read the fine print carefully. How much you're entitled to in a refund, if anything, if you move or change your mind. Know whether the price is guaranteed; know if any excess after your death will be given to your survivors."

Some pre-pay plans from the big firms are under challenge. SCI's Neptune Society program has been the subject of legal action in both Florida and California. A class-action suit launched in Florida in 2020 alleged that SCI attempted to sidestep state law, using a "bait and switch" scheme that involved pre-need payments for cremation. The suit claimed SCI's standard Neptune plan came with "high and hidden costs." In California, the attorney general's office alleged that the plan involved "unlawful business practices and systematic misconduct." It accused Neptune Society of pocketing more than $100 million, primarily from pre-need elderly customers. At last word, a decision was pending.

Studies of aggressive sales and pricing tactics employed by the funeral chains show just how effective they have been at driving up prices for consumers. A 2017 study by the US Bureau of Labor Statistics found that between December 1986 and September 2017, the cost of dying rose 227.1 percent, double the rate of all other consumer items (123.4 percent). The cost of burial caskets rose 230 percent over the same period while prices for wood and other commodities increased only 95 percent. Taking a longer view, the median cost of a funeral in the United States had increased from $708 in 1960 to $9,135 by 2019.

In the United Kingdom, the average basic funeral cost in 2020 was over £4,000 ($5,600), increasing to more than £9,000 ($12,600) when professional fees and discretionary extras such as memorials, flowers, and catering costs were included. That compares to £1,900 ($2,600) in the early 2000s.

Professors Samantha Fletcher and William McGowan, at universities in Manchester and Liverpool, respectively, maintain that the rising cost of death-care is becoming a huge burden for lower- and middle-class families. According to a study they authored in 2020, the funeral industry "has evolved in such a way that costs have risen continually, often in quite deliberate and manipulated ways." Huge corporate providers have "greedy shareholder mouths to feed," says McGowan, and "natural and commensurate supply and demand is too modest, financially speaking. So they have to work hard to create and capitalize on greater demand by not only pursuing the dead but targeting the living as well."

In the fourteen years prior to 2018, the cost of a basic funeral increased 6 percent annually. It is now high enough to eat up almost 40 percent of a low-income family's annual budget, and represents more than what they spend annually on food, energy, and clothing combined. "For many," says Fletcher, "the inability to pay these rising costs means the growth of personal debt and funeral poverty."

Fletcher and McGowan estimate the death-care sector in the United Kingdom has annual revenues of £2 billion. The largest funeral service provider in the market is Dignity PLC (the UK arm of SCI). It has more than 350 subsidiaries, most of them formerly independent morticians bought out by Dignity while retaining their traditional family-run names, and a total of 700 branches with plans for further expansion. Dignity is also the largest operator among the 283 crematoria in the United Kingdom.

A 2019 investigation by the UK Competition and Marketing Authority into soaring industry costs compared profits for Dignity with other UK operators, and companies in Europe, the United States, Canada, and Australia. Dignity recorded operating profits of between 19 and 26 percent, while those at Acorn AG in Germany and Park Lawn Corporation in Canada were between 13 and 16 percent. At last look (2021), SCI had a profit margin of 28 percent in 2021.

The phrase "you despicable beasts" was one of many pieces of consumer invective quoted by Fletcher and McGowan in their study. They found plenty of evidence of public outrage at the practices and expense of the death-care industry but also that policy makers tend to sidestep the issues. The burden on lower-income families raises the admittedly controversial question of whether the state should fund or subsidize death-care services. Whether such measures are warranted–or indeed, would be acceptable to the public–remains to be debated.

Based on the average funeral cost in the United Kingdom of £4,000, with half a million deaths annually, a national death-care program there could reach £200 billion ($235 billion) annually. This is relatively modest, McGowan suggests, compared to the National Health Service budget. "A national (death-care) service run for people over profit," he says, "could source and distribute materials and services at a much more competitive rate than the corporate sector if there was the political will to do so." It may be the sort of dramatic, systemic change required to bring the cost of dying back in line with the means of the living.

In the meantime, the United Kingdom's Competition and Market Authority has at least ruled that all funeral directors must display on their premises and websites a standard price list. They are also forbidden from paying hospitals, hospices, and care facilities for referrals, or for soliciting business through police officers or coroners.

The Federal Trade Commission advises consumers to "shop around, in advance. Compare prices from at least two funeral homes." Death-care advocate Shane Neufeld adds that people should ask a lot of questions of prospective suppliers, either when buying services at the time of need or in advance. Don't buy from someone who doesn't advertise their price list fairly and accurately, says Neufeld. And be careful of package discounts. "If I see a discount on a funeral home web site, that's everything I need to know," he says. "That's an indicator of what you're dealing with."

Nor should consumers be rushed into making decisions, even if a hospital or care facility is pressing for a decision on next steps. Urgency is not necessary, Neufeld says. Families can ask funeral homes to hold a body temporarily for a short time as they make plans. "There's nothing wrong with a funeral home saying they'll hold your relative for two to three days for $250 in a temperature-controlled environment," Neufeld explains. "And there's nothing wrong with a competing funeral home coming by to pick up the body. It happens all the time."

Families can also work the phones when someone is in the process of dying. "People sometimes feel funny about that," says Neufeld. "They feel like they're doing something disrespectful. But that's probably the best thing for themselves and the family. Don't feel odd or badly if you know the end is near. There's more time than people are led to believe." It doesn't mean you have to pre-pay, "but you should have your ducks in a row. Make sure you're comfortable with who you're dealing with."

Finally, challenge the necessity of each itemized good or service, and never be afraid to ask a funeral home what its markup is. "If they feel uncomfortable telling you," says Neufeld, "that's a problem."

Stephen Garrett, for his part, believes the industry has an important role to play in helping consumers navigate the death-care industry: "We believe if we educate all our citizens, they'll make the right choice." Of course, it's a challenge. "Our culture is very death averse," he says. "Nobody looks at it until their time of need and then it's almost too late."

Indeed, the cost of funerals is rarely, if ever, discussed within families or with others. Mentioning money matters at such a time seems almost to break a social taboo. But this reluctance prevents consumers from sharing information about price, service, and value, as they would with other, less less-important purchases.

The industry should indeed be proactive in reassuring consumers. Given the abundance of bad press, many are now suspicious of death-care practices, particularly those of the big funeral chains. Unless significant changes are made, more and more people will look to bypass the industry altogether.

CHAPTER FOURTEEN

Boomers at the brink

Enormous change in practices and attitudes towards death-care have taken place over the last century, from a time when almost everyone was buried in the earth to the rise of cremation as the preferred means of disposal to the present-day search for practical, affordable, dignified, and environmentally friendly alternatives. What will the next decades hold? What will the death-care field look like in 2040, the decade of departure? About the only thing we can say for certain is that there is more change coming. Boomers will put their own stamp on death and dying in the years ahead.

In *Our Changing Journey to the End*, Christina Staudt and J. Harold Ellens write that boomers are already rewriting the rules. "Boomers have been accused of, or commended for, taking innovative and even system-changing approaches towards almost every traditional or established pattern in the North American culture, and perhaps the worldwide social systems. Now they are applying their nonconformist approach to the management of their own dying."

The new approach will involve a shift in focus from old-fashioned ideas of avoiding death to efforts at controlling or managing it; from the notion of dying well, or a concentration on the process of dying, to a determination to live well until the end. The idea that "death is manageable" appeals to boomers, says Staudt: "They have been demanding control of their surroundings since their teenage years; and in their early old age they are determined to remain young. Barring the ability to hold death at bay, they intend to learn how to exit life as graciously and dignified as possible."

As a practical matter, that means boomers will want control over their health care and the balance of quality of live life versus longevity. They'll decide themselves if and how they want to live with chronic illnesses and dementia. Already, they are leading society towards "an increased interest in and innovative thought regarding assisted suicide," Ellens says. As of 2022, only ten states and the District of Columbia permit assisted suicide. More legal challenges are expected in the years ahead, along with a backlash against the procedure. (Canada's relatively liberal right-to-die laws were described in the Kansas City-based *National Catholic Reporter* this summer as "a frightening example of 'throwaway culture'.")

Boomers will also have strong ideas about funerals and methods of disposition, whether that means making all the decisions themselves or delegating them to children, family members, or others. Their approach is likely to involve "personalized final rites and funeral services" that honour the deceased and celebrate his or her life. "They are signing up by the thousands to MyWonderfulLife.com and taking positive initiative to plan their own style of celebrative funerals," writes Ellens, who expects the world will see more of "prepaid personalized commemorative ceremonies, shared electronic recording of simple tributes, online funerals instead of formal rituals."

As for disposition, boomers appear to be concerned with sharply reducing the expense of their leave-taking, writes Sara Marsden-Ille in US Funerals Online. "They may be the last generation to have the cash means to cover the cost of an impromptu funeral. And so many of this generation recognize the need to undertake some preplanning of their funeral arrangements. Not only to ensure that the costs can be met without burdening their children, but also to ensure that their wishes are met." That will likely keep simple cremation and other inexpensive options in the picture for generations to come. If they do decide to splurge a little on their funerals, says Marsden-Ille, they'll probably lean to acts of memorialization, which "appeal to the boomers' taste for personalization."

"Frequently I have seen an interesting sign in funeral par-
lors where I have conducted funerals of close acquaintances,"
Ellens says of the changing social values now hitting death-care.

It claims that the quality of a civilization can be discerned
best from the manner in which it treats and memorial-
izes its dead. I believe that is an accurate observation.
A century ago, in the culture of my childhood, that would
have implied forthrightly that the only civilized way to
conduct the journey to our end is to celebrate the life of
the deceased in a heroic commemoration and a solemn
but dramatic funeral. Any suggestion at that time that the
entire matter might be significantly truncated by a cremation and brief memorial service with only the nuclear
family attending would have been considered uncivilized
and disrespectful. That is no longer the case and it is now
difficult to find believable social or spiritual reasons to
value negatively such an abbreviated completion of our
attention to our loved ones. Boomers in general do not
see that such an efficient and cost-saving approach would
be inadequately loving or estimable for themselves. More
practical is apparently more perfect for that generation
now coming to the point of thinking about their own
demise. . . . Apparently it is becoming preferable to die than
to become psychologically or economically burdensome
to loved ones.

Where does all this end up? Ellens sketches three possible scenarios. First, the boomers lead us to an increasingly secular world in which any notion of an afterlife is dismissed and "the management of death is merely the rather trivial matter of disposal of the worthless remains of a life that is already erased." That spells an end for the rather elaborate funeral culture that has held sway in recent centuries.

A second possibility is that the boomers double down on their long-standing interest in otherworldly matters and become so preoccupied with spiritual fulfilment and personal transcendence that they lose interest in what becomes of their physical remains. That, too, would mean a radical departure from funeral culture as their parents and grandparents understood it.

Ellens' third and most intriguing possibility is that the boomers as a cohort triumph over the historic human struggle with death anxiety. This takes us back to thanatophobia, or unreasonable fear of death. Psychologists describe it as anxiety caused by exposure to a situation related to death. A person so diagnosed develops obsessive behaviours and ideas around the deadline of death, for his or herself, and for others. It is manifested by clinical signs and often leads to avoidance behaviours, or what Freud called death denial.

The American Psychiatric Association doesn't officially recognize thanatophobia as a disorder. It says that the anxiety towards death some people face is usually attributable to general anxiety disorder. While it is natural for someone to worry about his or her own health as the years go by, or to worry about friends and family as they approach the end, most people in fact worry less as their time approaches. William Chopik, a professor of psychology at Michigan State University, surveyed 2,300 adults and discovered that with exposure to death and the likelihood of it coming closer, death-related thoughts and anxiety actually decline across a person's lifespan.

Another expert, psychologist Robert Kastenbaum, found that empirical studies of death anxiety reveal that most people have a low to moderate level of death-related anxiety. He, too, found that death anxiety, if anything, declines as people age. Women tend to report somewhat higher levels than men (their concerns are often focused on others rather than themselves). People with mental and emotional disorders tend to have more death anxiety than the general population, while higher levels of education and socio-economic status are modestly related to lower levels. Death anxiety can spike temporarily for people who have been exposed to traumatic situations. Finally, religious faith and practices sometimes reduce and sometimes increase these feelings.

Boomers, ventures Ellens, might be clearheaded and confident enough to have "no particular anxiety or sense of obligation regarding rituals of farewell." They are, after all, "the generation that started early to act in an antiestablishment style, defying the constraints of ideal social decorum, repudiating the heroic traditions of their parents, and generally revolting against all restrains on their radical individual freedom and narcissism. Insofar as that worked for them, it may well have given them a sense of self-confidence that also removes all historic notions about traditional styles of death rituals as well as traditional notions of eternity." This is yet another reason to believe that however boomers ultimately decide to make their exits, it will be on their own terms, and with scant regard for precedent or the traditional offerings of the funeral industry.

Of course, there is always something artificial about generalizations. Boomers, in fact, are a diverse lot, representing a vast array of social and cultural values, spiritual faiths, and familial and community connections. There is no logical reason why all three of Ellens' scenarios couldn't play out to some extent. By 2040, some people may still be choosing conventional ground burials and elaborate church funerals, while others will be opting for methods of disposal and memorialization that haven't occurred to us yet.

But if there is one value that binds the boomers together more than any other, says author Robert McCrum, it is personal autonomy, the validation of the self, the right to choose. McCrum is the author of *Every Third Thought: On Life, Death, and the Endgame*, which takes its title from Prospero's lines in Shakespeare's *The Tempest*: "And thence retire me to my Milan, where/Every third thought shall be my grave."

McCrum believes that the one thing boomers will want more than a particular coffin or ceremony or means of disposal will be a narrative that guides one to the finish. Some will find it in the church, some in literature or philosophy, some in folklore or music or popular culture or relationships. "Consoling narratives," he says, "must be patched together from transient fragments of experience."

Ed Bixby, the green burial guru in the United States, agrees that the way in which we frame death is important. Contemporary society, he says, has become removed from the processes of death, which now occur more often in a hospital or hospice than a home. Professionals have supplanted family and friends in caring for the deceased. Baby boomers, he says, may lead us to a greater acceptance of death than we've known for some time.

"We can allow the death of someone to be the final statement of a life that was lived," Bixby says, with the funeral serving as a celebration of the individual. By letting people depart on their own terms, fulfilling their own narratives, "we can relieve some of the burden, make hearts a little less heavy."

That boomers are unlikely to demand traditional burial plots and don't want to spend much on their down disposition will undoubtedly present challenges for parts of the funeral industry, but some death-care providers are already pivoting to capitalize on the emerging trend towards personal death narratives.

The Neptune Society, one of the most aggressive pre-sellers of funeral arrangements, is telling boomers that they "might not want to be remembered lying stiffly in a casket in the impersonal atmosphere of a funeral home. Instead, you might prefer to be remembered as a loving and caring person. You might want your unique life to be recognized and celebrated by all of your loved ones and friends." That is part of a pitch for personalized cremation services, which come with the options of individualized urns shaped and decorated to your specifications, ash-scattering ceremonies, custom jewellery made from small amounts of ashes, and so on. To get around boomer sensitivity to placing economic burdens on others, Neptune is also pushing pre-payment as a means to avoid burdening children and relations.

Other service providers have leaned further into appeals to boomer self-affirmation. Alavida, a division of Montreal's Kane & Fetterly Funeral Home, headlines its marketing page, "It's My Party and I'll Die Like I Want To." Death, according to Alavida, is indeed a party: "To the boomer, the urge to live and die as they want is reshaping the very nature of funeral services . . . thanks to boomers' distaste for the sombre doom and gloom ceremonies. More boomers are opting for fun, party-like funerals and elaborate services."

Alavida offers online cremation arrangements and inter-active memorial tributes. It claims that rock music will become a mainstay at funerals, as will ceremonies in remote and beautiful outdoor settings "with the deceased buried in an environmentally-friendly cardboard urn that turns them into a tree." Its website presents the company as a party planner more than a funeral parlour, with packages including audiovisual equipment, décor and table styling, music and entertainment, photographers and videographers, food and beverage provision–everything but a red carpet.

These trends aren't limited to North America. Poppy's Funerals in London advertises itself as a funeral home "on a mission to give people the funeral they want, need, and can feel proud of." The firm emphasizes adding "meaning and personality" to ceremonies, and prioritizing choice, flexibility, and access to information. A UK survey of co-op funeral directors found that half of them had arranged a service somewhere other than a crematorium or church in the previous twelve months, reflecting the rise of the "destination funeral." These might be at a favourite restaurant, bar, beach, or bowling alley. Requests that funeral guests wear non-black clothes are increasingly common. Hearses are being replaced with buses, motorcycles, and horse-drawn carriages.

Poppy is an example of a new breed of "death concierge" that *Forbes* magazine credits with disrupting the billion-dollar funeral industry. Together with like-minded entrepreneurs, it will steer boomers away from stiff, fussy, and conventional options to a world in which the deceased plays the role of funeral director, choosing the venue and the soundtrack and the speakers, the look and feel of the occasion, and putting his or her life story and values on display. Far from a gloomy or morbid affair, this last dance will be the crowning achievement of a person's life, effectively writing the last page of the all-important personal narrative.

There will still be a body requiring disposition no matter how grand or celebratory the leave-taking. Still, it's not difficult to imagining a coming world in which the disposal of the body might be an afterthought. Some death-care providers even now are offering a whole other range of end-of-life services, including management of home sales, getting rid of furniture and household effects, archiving photos, closing down social media accounts, among other chores. Disposition of the body may wind up as just another task on the checklist, and not a terribly consequential one at that.

Postscript

"Why do people have to die?" That was the question put by a bereaved family member to funeral director Nate Fisher in the aforementioned award-winning HBO series *Six Feet Under*, praised as "an unexpectedly beautiful rumination on life, death and grief." After pausing a moment to grasp a spark of wisdom, Nate responded in the most profound manner he could muster: "To make life important. None of us knows how long we've got, which is why we have to make each day matter. A life well-lived . . . that's the most any of us can hope for."

When we are young, we think we'll never age, much less reach the ends of our days. We expect we'll have countless years to make crucial decisions about our lives and plan for our dotage. We are more inclined to wonder if our existence is as good as it might be than to recognize what a precious gift life is. But our time is not limitless. Even the wealthiest of us can't buy more of it. And the end can come unexpectedly, leaving us without opportunity for contemplation.

Our days, then, should not be taken for granted. They should be treasured for their great value. And so should our deaths because, as the novelist Haruki Murakami says, "death is not the opposite of life but a part of it."

If you have made the time to read this book, I encourage you to give serious thought to your inevitable end. The choices available to you may be limited or not, depending on your circumstances, but they are always complex, requiring an inventory of one's values, concerns, desires, and responsibilities. This book has been intended to help you answer some complex questions, and also to pose more of them. The rest is up to you.

Helpful Resources

Some valuable observations on death:

"Even death is not to be feared by one who has live life wisely."
—Buddha, fourth-fifth century BC.

"Our death is our wedding with eternity."
—Rumi, thirteenth-century Islamic poet and mystic.

"If you don't know how to die, don't worry; Nature will tell you what to do on the spot, fully and adequately. She will do this job perfectly for you; don't bother your head about it."
—Michel de Montaigne, sixteenth-century French philosopher

"It seems to me most strange that men should fear, seeing that death, a necessary end. Will come when it will come."
—William Shakespeare.

"Our dead are never dead to us, until we have forgotten them."

–George Eliot

"The fear of death follows from the fear of life. A man who lives fully is prepared to die at any time."

–Mark Twain

"Death is not the end. There remains the litigation over the estate."

–Ambrose Pierce, American writer, journalist, poet, and Civil War veteran.

"If you wish to be remembered, then leave a lot of debts."

–Elbert Hubbard, American writer, artist, and philosopher.

"One never knows the ending. One has to die to know what exactly happens after death, although Catholics have their hopes."

–Alfred Hitchcock, filmmaker.

"Live as if you were to die tomorrow. Learn as if you were to live forever."

–Mohandas (Mahatma) Gandhi.

"Do not seek death. Death will find you. But seek the road that makes death a fulfillment."
–Dag Hammarskjöld, UN Secretary-General 1953–1961.

"Old friends pass away, new friends appear. It is just like the days. An old day passes, a new day arrives. The important thing is to make it meaningful."
–Tenzin Gyato, Dalai Lama.

"I have lived with the prospect of an early death for the last forty-nine years. I'm not afraid of death, but I'm in no hurry to die. I regard the brain as a computer which will stop working when its components fail. There is no heaven or afterlife for broken down computers; that is a fairy story for people afraid of the dark."
–Stephen Hawking

"Death is a destination we all share. No one has the ever escaped it, and that is as it should be, because death is very likely the single invention of life. It clears out the old and makes way for the new."
–Steve Jobs

Books

A partial list of some of the best books on the subject of end-of-life, the death-care industry, and the problems and management of grief. Be warned that many were published several years ago and do not include the latest information on alternative disposition methods.

- *The American Way of Death Revisited* by Jessica Mitford. "A funny and unforgiving book is the best memento mori we are like to get. It should be updated and reissued each decade"–*New York Review of Books* (First Vintage Books, Reprint ed. 1998).
- *Confessions of a Funeral Director: How Death Saved My Life* by Caleb Wilde. "Humans are biologically wired to evade death for as long as possible, we have become too adept at hiding it, vilifying it, and–when it can no longer be avoided–letting the professionals take over" (HarperOne, 2018).
- *All the Ways Our Dead Still Speak: A Funeral Director on Life, Death and the Hereafter* by Caleb Wilde. "A lyrical and tender quest to encounter the hereafter" (Broadleaf Books, 2022).
- *Final Rights: Reclaiming the American Way of Death* by Joshua Slocum and Lisa Carlson. Prominent leaders of the funeral consumer movement, Slocum, executive director

of Funeral Consumers Alliance, and Lisa Carlson, director of Funeral Ethics Organization, expose wrongdoing,
inform consumers of their rights, and propose legal
reforms (Upper Access Inc., 2011).

- *The Profits of Death: An Insider Exposes the Death Care
Industries* by Darryl J. Roberts. "I can't think of a better
person to blow the whistle in the funeral industry"–Lisa
Carlson (Five Star Publications, 1997).

- *Caring for the Dead: Your Final Act of Love* by Lisa Carlson.
A guide for making funeral arrangements with or without
a funeral director. "The most comprehensive book over
produced in this subject," says John F. Wasik, *Consumers
Digest* (Upper Access Book Pub., 1997).

- *Elderhood: Redefining Aging, Transforming Medicine,
Reimagining Life* by Louise Aronson. Finalist for the
Pulitzer Prize in general non-fiction and *New York Times*
bestseller. Physician and award-winning author Aronson
offers stories from twenty-five years of caring for her
patients (Bloomsbury Publishing, Reprint ed. 2021).

- *Our Last Best Act: Planning for the End of Our Lives to Protect
the Places and People We Love* by Mallory McDuff. Bridges
the gap between environmental action and religious faith
by demonstrating that when the two are combined, they
become a powerful force (Broadleaf Books, 2021).

- *Death to Dust* by Kenneth Iverson, MD. A book that provides answers what everyone wants to ask about what

happens to dead bodies in a question-and-answer format. (Glen Press, 1994)

- *A Beginner's Guide to the End: Practical Advice for Living Life and Facing Death* by Dr. B.J. Miller and Shoshana Berger. "A gentle, knowledgeable guide to a fate we all share," says the *Washington Post* (Simon and Schuster, 2020).

- *Is the Cemetery Dead?* by David Charles Sloane. New and evolving rituals and the future of the cemetery (University of Chicago Press, 2018)

- *The Baby Boom: How It Got That Way, and It Wasn't My Fault, and I'll Never Do It Again* by P.J. O'Rourke. The late American humourist (1947-2022) takes a caustic and tongue-in-cheek look at his generation. "O'Rourke finds much to deplore in the boomer character, but even more to cherish and celebrate"-*Chicago Tribune* (Atlantic Monthly Press, 2014).

- *The Art of Dying Well: A Practical Guide to a Good End of Life* by Katy Butler. "Makes the most intimidating of processes come across as approachable"-*Publishers Weekly* (Scribner, Reprint ed. 2019).

- *Grave Matters* by Mark Harris. A journey through the modern industry to a natural, more economical, and meaningful alternative to the conventional funeral parlour (Scribner, Reprint ed. 2008).

- *Rest in Peace: Insider's Tips to the Low Cost, Low Stress Funeral* by Brian Burkhardt. Walks readers through the funeral situation and offers step-by-step solutions for planning (Morgan James Publishing, 2008).

- *The Green Burial Guidebook: Everything You Need to Plan an Affordable, Environmentally Friendly Funeral* by Elizabeth Fournier. "Lovely, thoughtful, and beautifully crafted"–Mary Woodsen, Green Burial Council (New World Library, 2018).
- *Greening Death: Reclaiming Burial Practices and Restoring Our Tie to the Earth* by Suzanne Kelly. Reclaiming old practices in new ways for a new age (Rowman & Littlefield Publishers, 2017).
- *When Death Speaks* by Stephen Garrett. Changing the conversation around death to one of openness and inspiration (FriesenPress, 2013).
- *On Death and Dying: What the Dying Have to Teach Doctors, Nurses, Clergy and Their Own Families* by Elisabeth Kübler-Ross. Updated fifty years after its original publication, Dr. Kübler-Ross's beloved, ground breaking classic on the five stages of grief. One of the most important psychological studies of twentieth century (Scribner, Reissued 2014).
- *The Art of Dying* by Peter and Elizabeth Fenwick. A book to help the dying, their loved ones, and their health-care workers better understand the dying process and come to terms with death itself. Neuropsychiatrist Peter Fenwick believes consciousness may survive the death of the brain (Continuum, 2008).

- *Being Mortal: Medicine and What Matters in the End* by Atul Gawande. How medicine can not only improve life but also the process of its ending (Metropolitan Books, 2014).

- *Click Here When I Die: Making Things Easier for Those You Love* by Jonathan S. Braddock. "Leaving a mess behind for your family and friends can be avoided. They can rest easy, and you can rest in peace" (Lioncrest, 2017).

- *Talking about Death Won't Kill You: The Essential Guide to End-of-Life Conversations* by Dr. Kathy Kortes-Miller. Handbook to help navigate personal and medical decisions for the best quality of life at the end of life (ECW Press, 2018).

- *Embracing Grief: Leaning Into Loss to Find Life* by Alise Chaffins. Examines the author's life as impacted by grief and how she learned to live more fully (Self-published, 2015).

- *A Decent Life: Morality for the Rest of Us* by Todd May. Presents philosophical concepts in ways that are easily graspable (University of Chicago Press, 2019).

- *The Good Funeral* by Thomas Long and Thomas Lynch. Discusses challenges of the "good funeral," including the commercial aspects that have led many to be suspicious of funeral directors (Westminster John Knox Press, 2013).

- *A Good Goodbye: Funeral Planning for Those Who Don't Plan to Die* by Gail Rubin. Deals with "the importance of funeral planning and being best prepared for the inevita ble deaths we will have to deal with in our lives"–Funeral Consumers Alliance (Light Tree Press, 2010).

- *The Work of the Dead: A Cultural History of Mortal Remains* by Professor Thomas W. Laqueur. A compelling and detailed account of how and why the living have cared for the dead, from antiquity to the twentieth century (Princeton University Press, 2015).

Other books quoted: *A Short History of Nearly Everything* by Bill Bryson; *Boom, Bust & Echo* by David K. Foot; *Empty Planet* by Darrell Bricker & and John Ibbitson; *From Beginning to End* by Robert Fulghum; *Heat Wave* by Eric Klinenberg.

Websites

Confessions of a Funeral Director (Caleb Wilde blog): https:// www.calebwilde.com

Seven Ponds, El Cerrito (Albany), California: www.sevenponds. com

People's Memorial Association: https://peoplesmemorial.org

Green Burial Council (United States and Canada): https:// www.greenburialcouncil.org

Funeral Consumers Alliance: https://funerals.org/consumers/

Final Passages: https://finalpassages.org

National Home Funeral Alliance: homefuneralalliance.org

The Canadian Integrative Network for Death Education and Alternatives: http://cindea.ca/home-funerals.html

US Funeral Online: https://www.us-funerals.com/

The Funeral Rule (US Federal Trade Commission): https://www.consumer.ftc.gov/articles/0300-ftc-funeral-rule

National Funeral Directors Association (US): https://nfda.org

Funeral Association of Canada: https://www.fsac.ca

National Society of Allied and Independent Funeral Directors (UK): https://saif.org.uk

National Association of Funeral Directors (UK): https://www.nafd.org.uk

Funeral Trade Associations: https://beyond.life/help-centre/admin-legal/funeral-trade-associations-nafd-saif/

American Association of Retired Persons: www.aarp.org/home-family/caregiving/

National Institute on Aging: https://www.nia.nih.gov/health/what-do-after-someone-dies

Funeral Help Center: www.funeralhelpcenter.com

Ethical Death Care (Winnipeg, Manitoba): www.ethicaldeathcare.com

Dying with Dignity: https://www.dyingwithdignity.ca/

In the Light Turns: https://inthelightturns.com

"The Art of Dying Well," TED talk by Dr. Peter Fenwick: https://www.youtube.com/watch?v=U-CXpReUpiM

Dying Matters: www.dyingmatters.org

Death Doulas:

https://endoflifedoulaassociation.org/

http://www.bioethics.net/2019/11/making-death-doulas-
mainstream-a-struggle-between-tradition-and-modernity/

http://www.nedalliance.org/

https://www.aarp.org/caregiving/home-care/info-2018/end-
of-life-doulas.html

Federation of Burial and Cremation Authorities: https://www.
fbca.org.uk/

Home Funeral Directory: www.homefuneralalliance.org

Body Donation: donatelifeamerica@donatelife.net

Green Burial Society of Canada: http://www.greenburialcanada.
ca/

Funeral Advisory and Memorial Society: https://www.fams.ca

Memorial Society of BC: https://memorialsocietybc.org/

Organ Donation: www.livingbank.org, www.giftoflife.on.ca/
en/aboutus.htm

The Canadian Integrative Network for Death Education and
Alternatives: http://cindea.ca/home-funerals.html

Federation des Cooperatives due Quebec : https://www.fcfq.
coop/

Social Security Administration: www.ssa.gov

Death Benefit: https://www.canada.ca/en/services/benefits/
publicpensions/cpp/cpp-death-benefit.html

Acknowledgements

Thanks to publisher Ken Whyte of Sutherland House, who recognized the growing importance of this subject, for his valuable advice, know-how, and contributions. Without his guidance this book might never have seen the light of day.

My special thanks to Linda Sutton, retired *Toronto Star* senior editor, University of Western Ontario journalism grad and my patient and dedicated in-house content advisor, copy editor, and proofreader, without whom I might never have reached a final draft.

Also, to the more than 150 sources contacted on four continents over four years for their invaluable knowledge, insights, and comments, many of them included here: Prof. Carlton Basmajian (Iowa State University); Ed Bixby (Green Burial Council); Barbara Kemmis (Cremation Association of North America); Amanda Stock and Nora Menkin (People's Memorial Association); Erik Lees (landscape architect/Green Burial Society of Canada); Josh Slocum (Funeral Consumers Alliance);

Lisa Carlson (Funeral Consumers Alliance/Funeral Ethics Organization); Dr. Eric Striessnig (International Institute. for Applied Systems Analysis, Vienna); Leora Courtney-Wolfman (University of Vienna); Rev. Stephen Garrett (end-of-life coach); Shane Neufeld (death-care consultant); Christina Staudt (Columbia University); Darrell Bricker (Ipsos Public Affairs); David K. Foot (demographer); Caleb Wilde (funeral director); Drew Gray (funeral director); Trevor Charbonneau (funeral director); Sandy Mahon (Funeral and Cremation Services Council of Saskatchewan), Joe Wilson (Bio-Response Solutions); Sandy Sullivan (Resomation Ltd.); Sister Renée Mirkes, PhD (Franciscan Sisters of Christian Charity); Mary Nash (green burial advocate); Bob Hendrikx (LOOP Biotech); Laura Green (toxicologist); Philip Olson (Virginia Polytechnic Institute.); Dr. Gerald Denys (microbiologist); Drs. Thomas Champney, Callum Ross, Ann Zumwalt, Bruce Wainman, Edwin Moore, and Leslie MacKenzie (anatomy laboratory directors); Terry Regnier (Mayo Clinic); Prof. William McGowan (University of Liverpool); Dr. Susan Fletcher (Manchester University); Susan Greer (Natural Burial Association); Walt Patrick (Herland Forest Cemetery); Pat Ottmann (*Canadian Funeral News*); Dr. Patrick Gerland (United Nations Population Division); Paul Harris (Regulatory Support Services); Suzette Sherman (SevenPonds.com); Louis Grenier (funeral co-operative, Calgary); Andy Kollmorgen, (CHOICE consumer advocacy group, Australia); David Brazeau (Bereavement Authority of

Ontario); Prof. Christopher Coutts (Florida State University); Dr. Troy Hottle (Eastern Research Group); Susanne/Peter Wiigh-Mäsak (Promessa Organic AB); Dr. Pierre Gosselin (Quebec Health Institute.); US Census Bureau; Jonathan Chagnon (Statistics Canada); UK Office for National Statistics.

Index